I0476069

Pandamania!

© 2014 by Francis Gonn
Illustrated by Francis Gonn
All rights reserved

ISBN-13: 978-1502393586
ISBN-10: 1502393581

The author and illustrator, Francis Gonn, loves pandas and as a hobby during his retirement years. After a career as a design architect, he made drawings for a series of children books from which many of these caricatures have appeared.

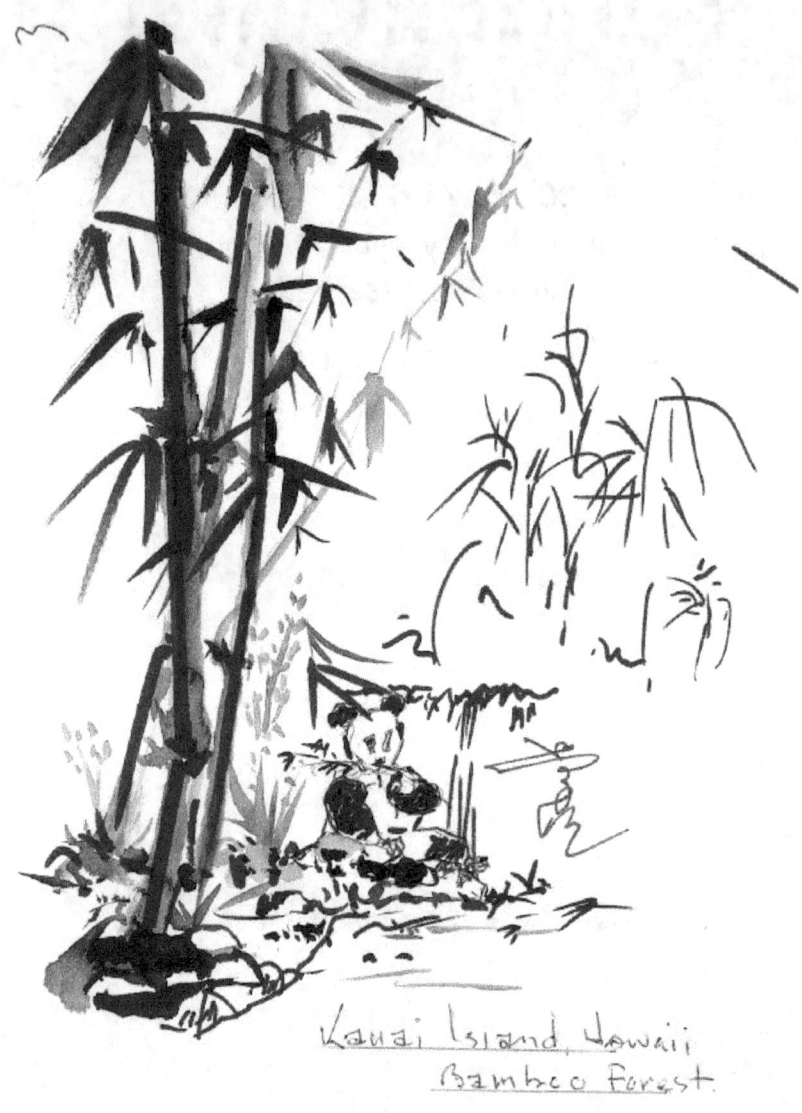

A panda enjoys eating bamboo leaves.

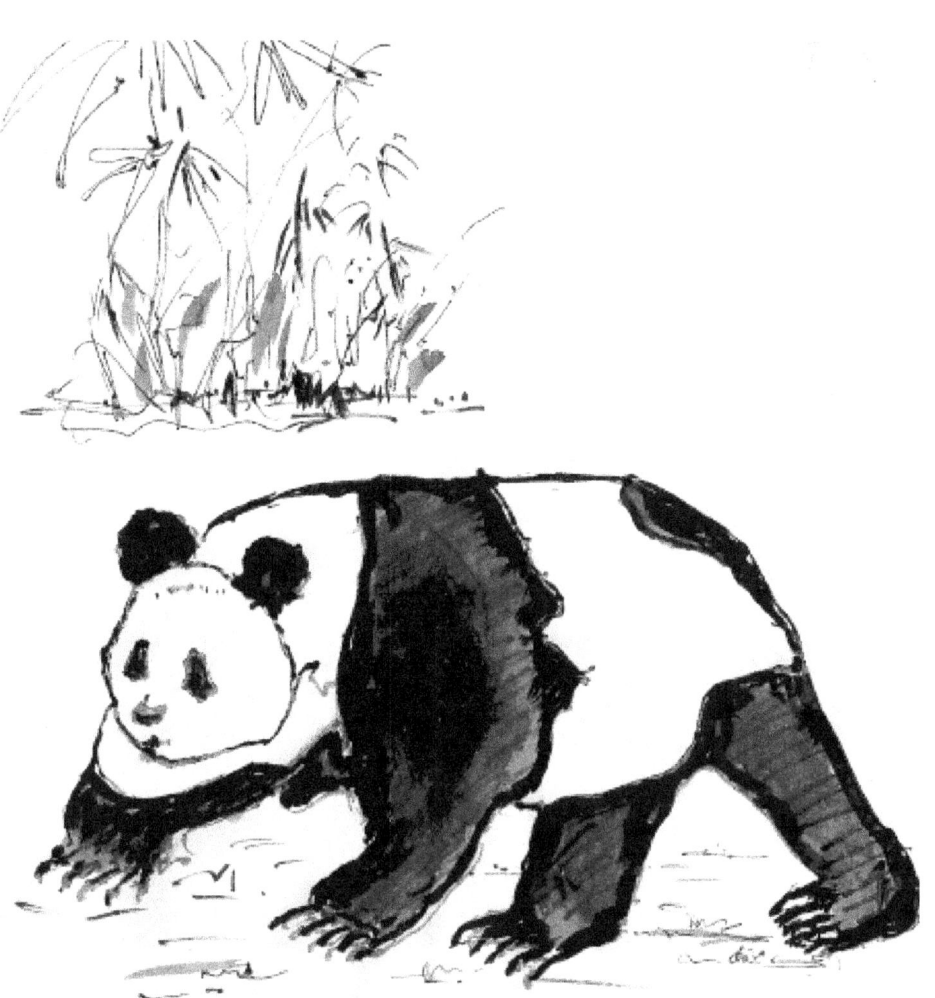

Big daddy panda marks his territory.

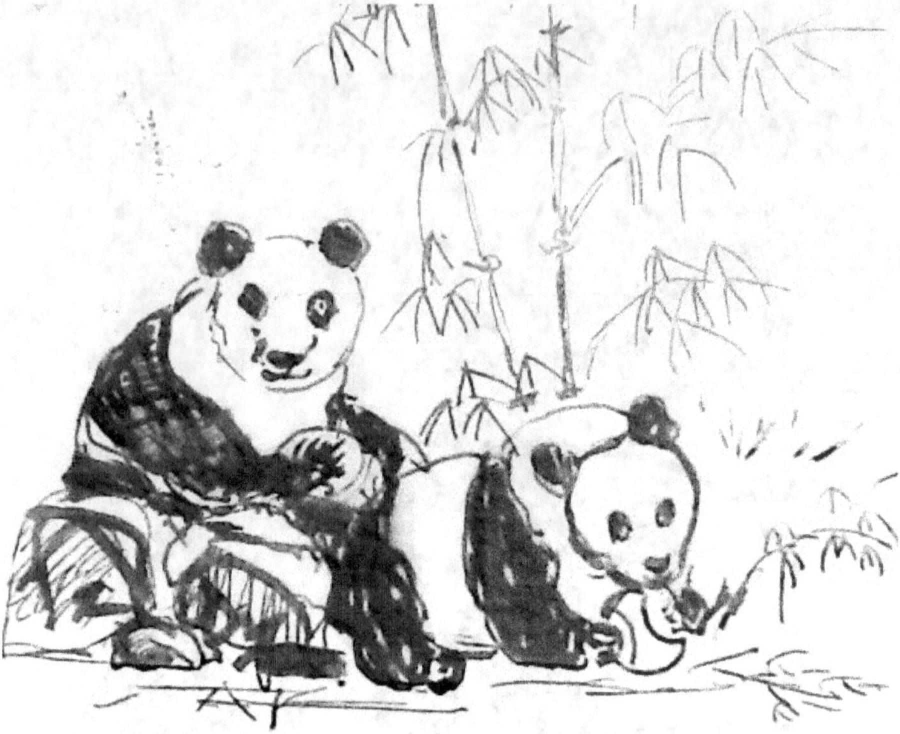

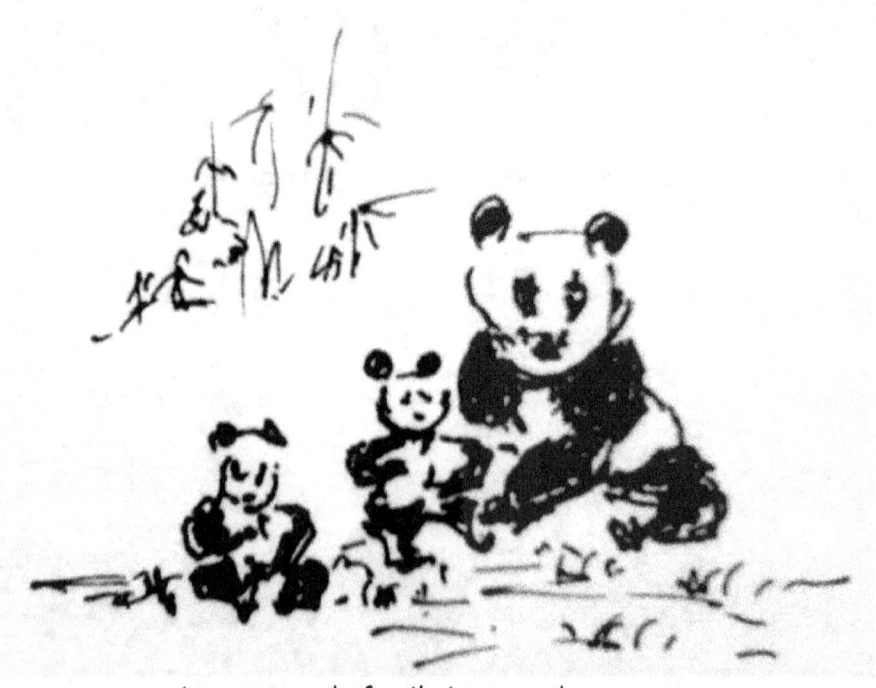

Pandas enjoy sweet melons

A young panda family in a meadow

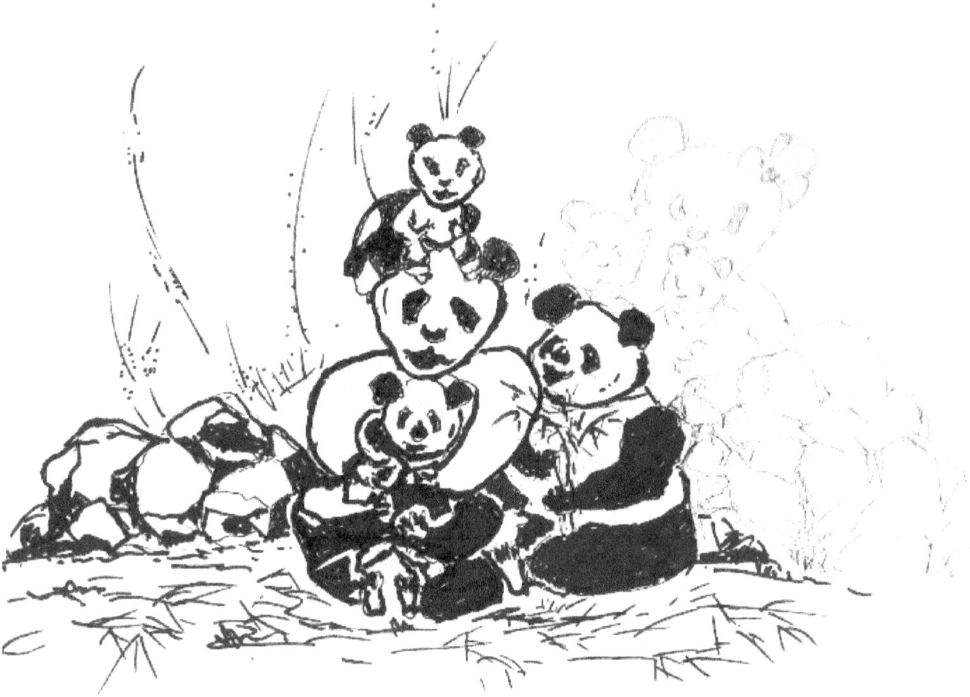

A happy panda family

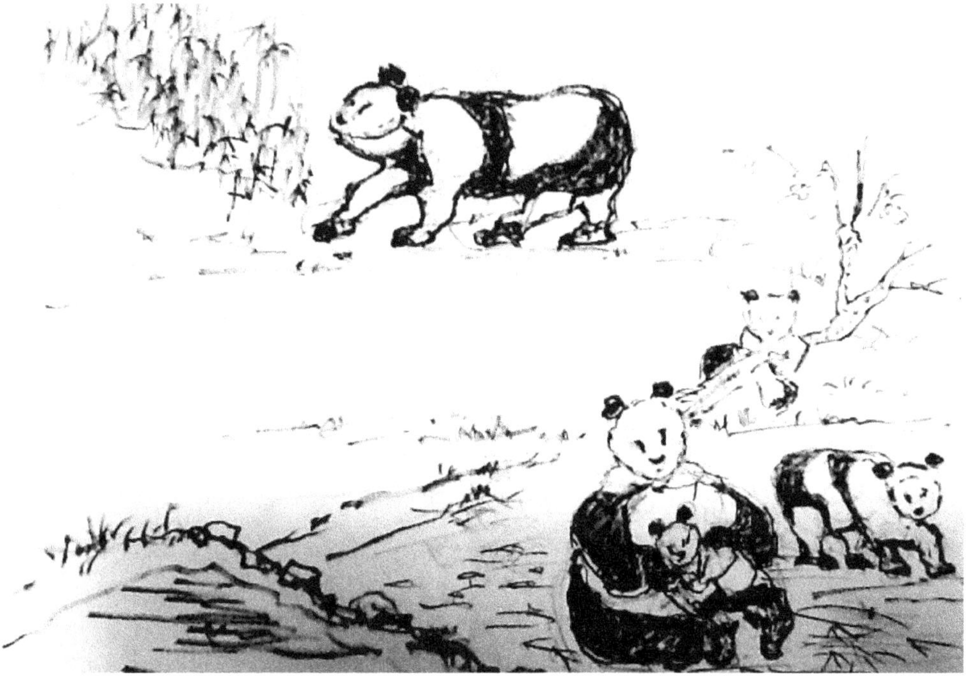

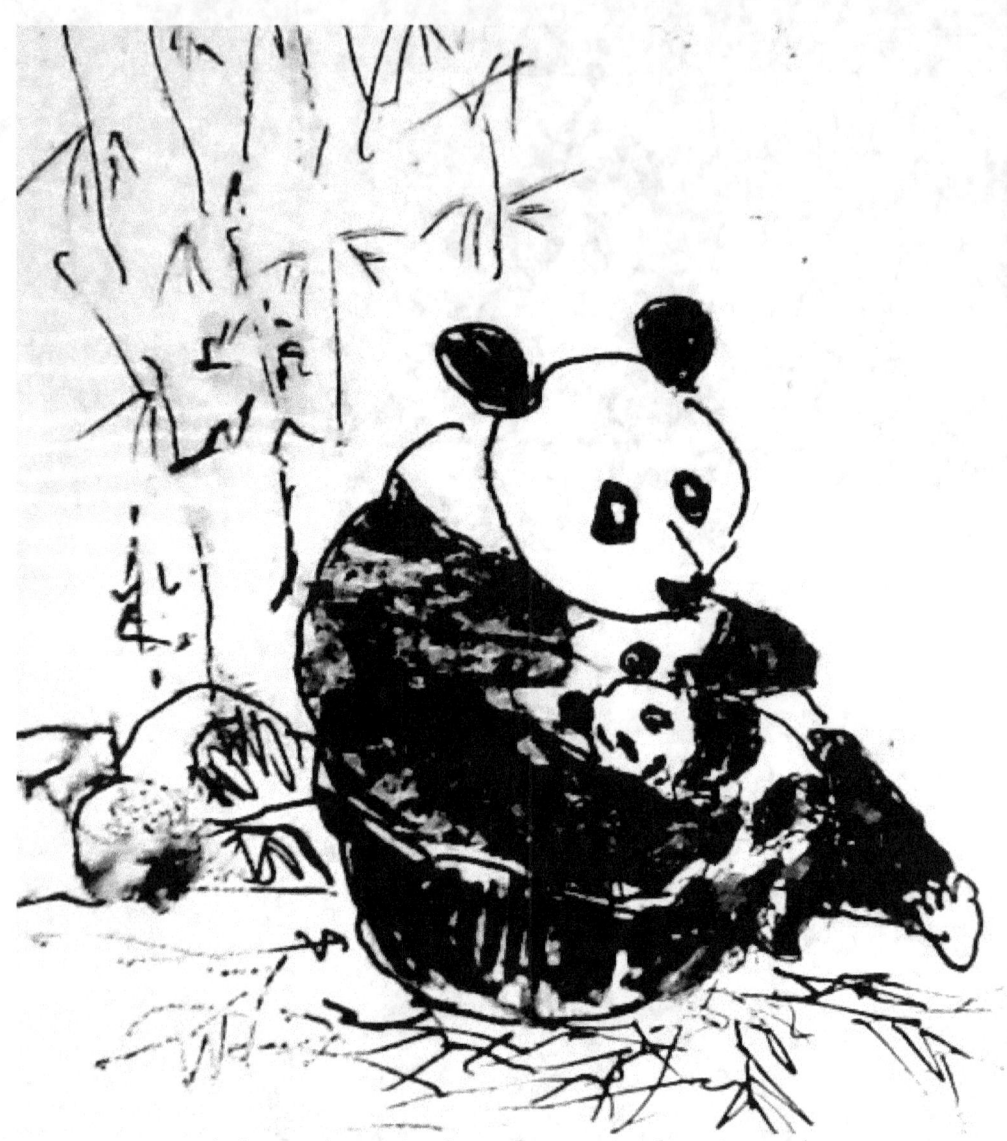

A baby panda getting lots of attention from its mother

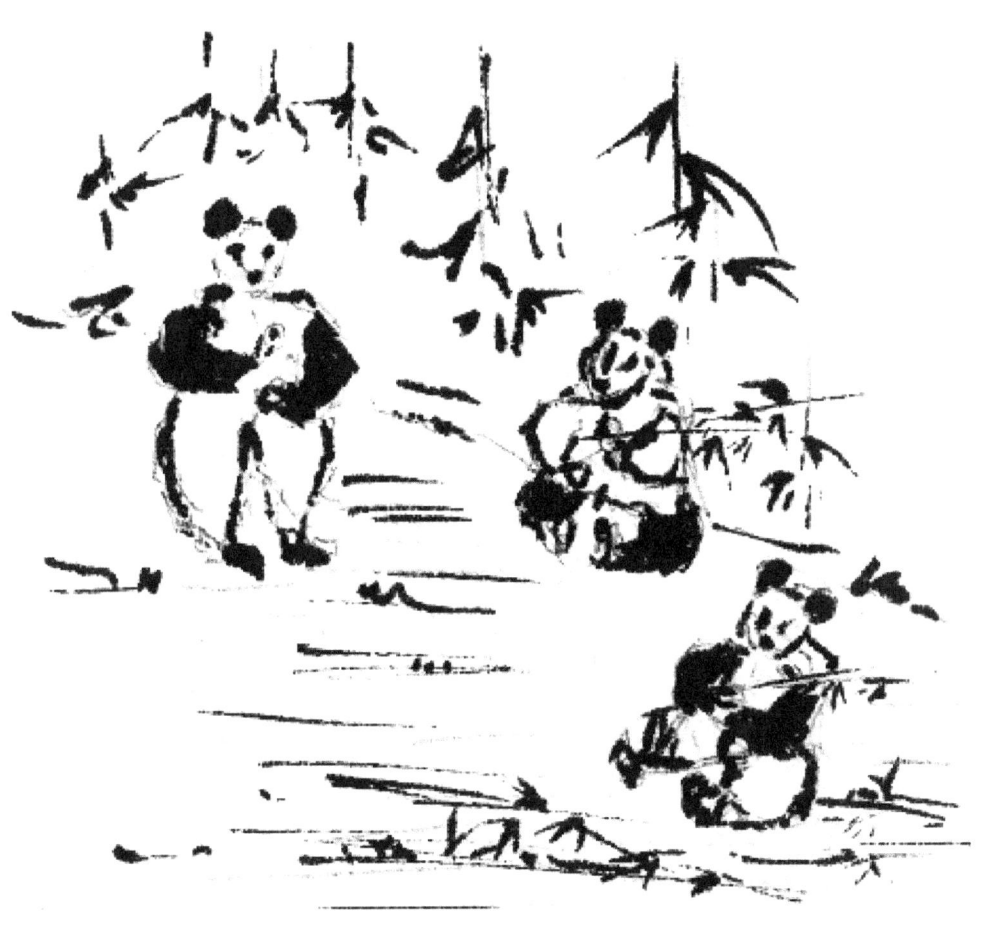

A panda family enjoys a bamboo snack break.

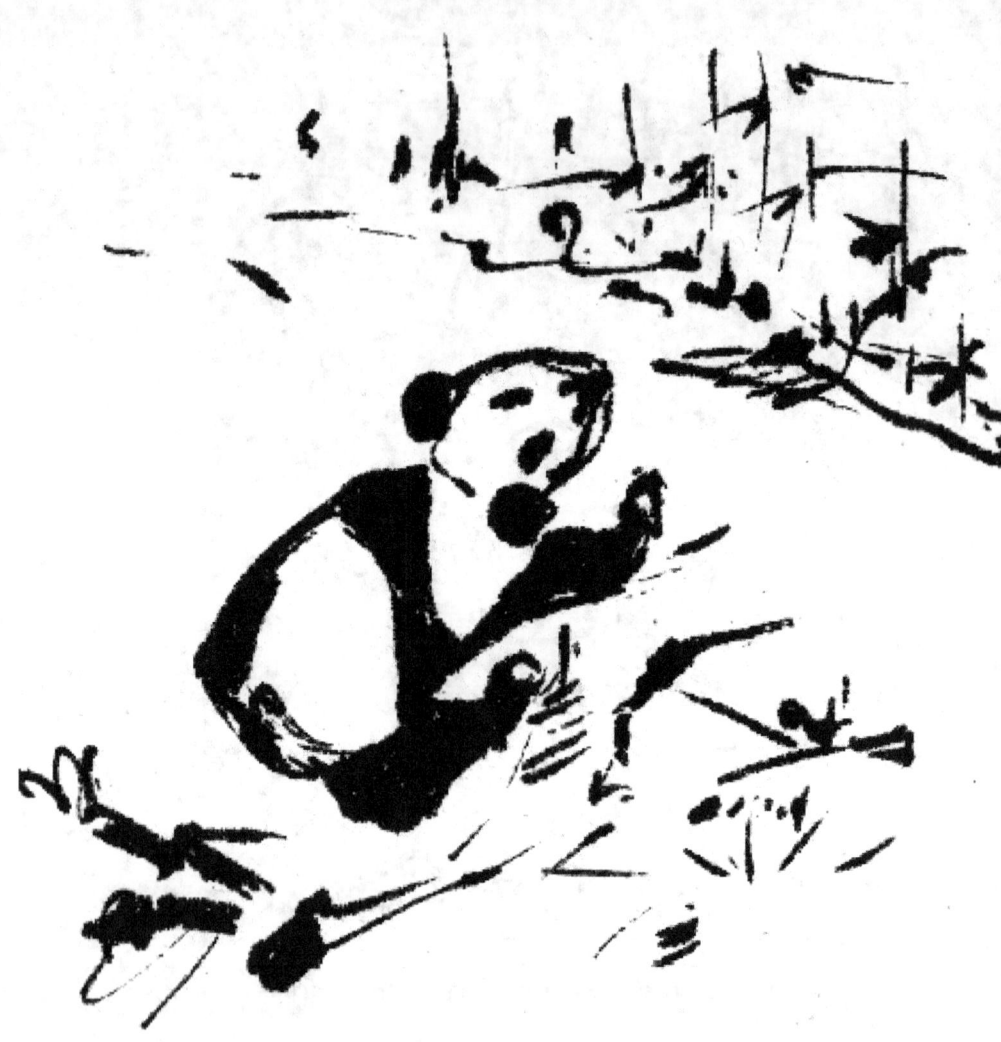

A lone panda sniffing for the scent of human poachers.

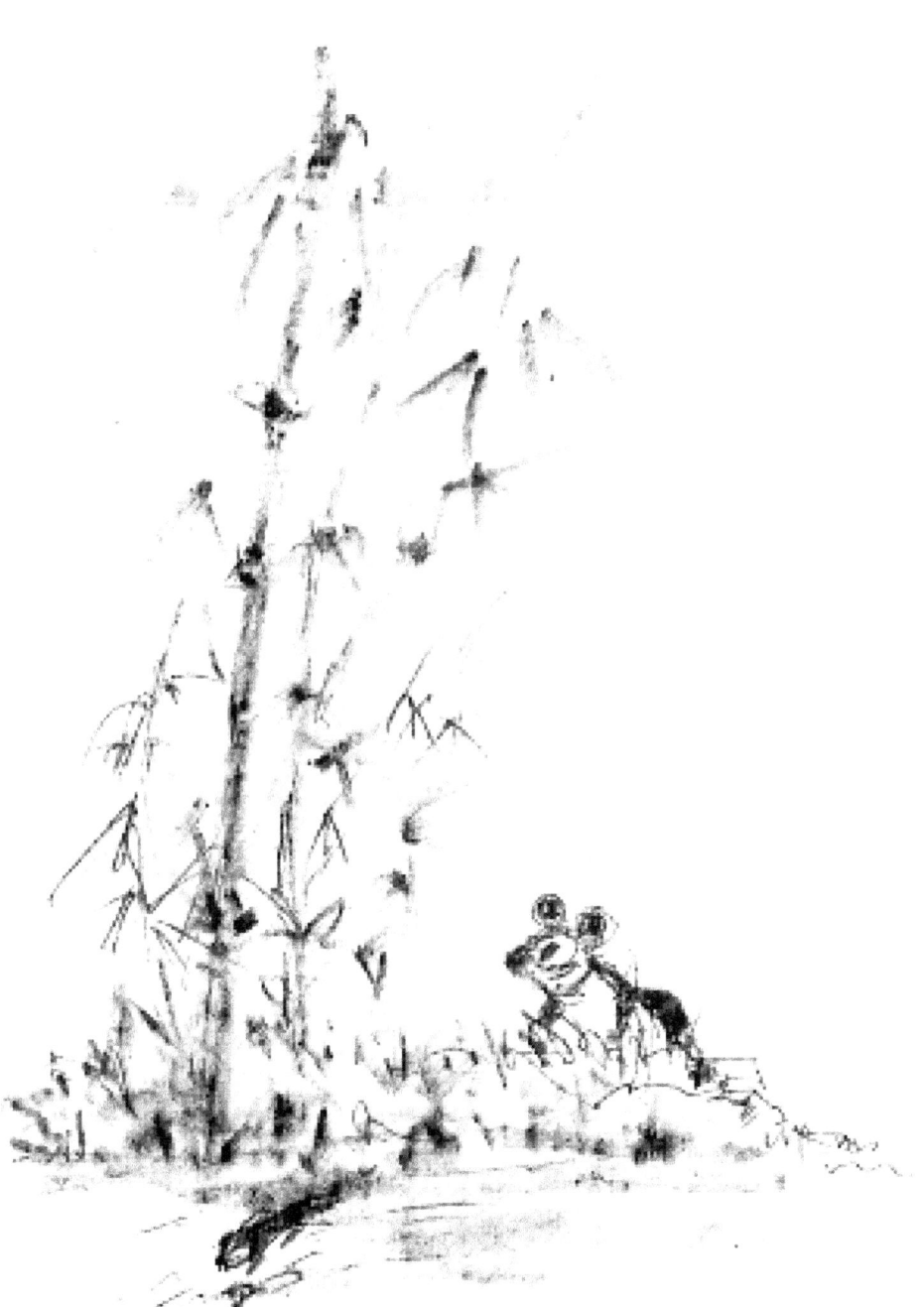

A panda spots another fresh bamboo meal.

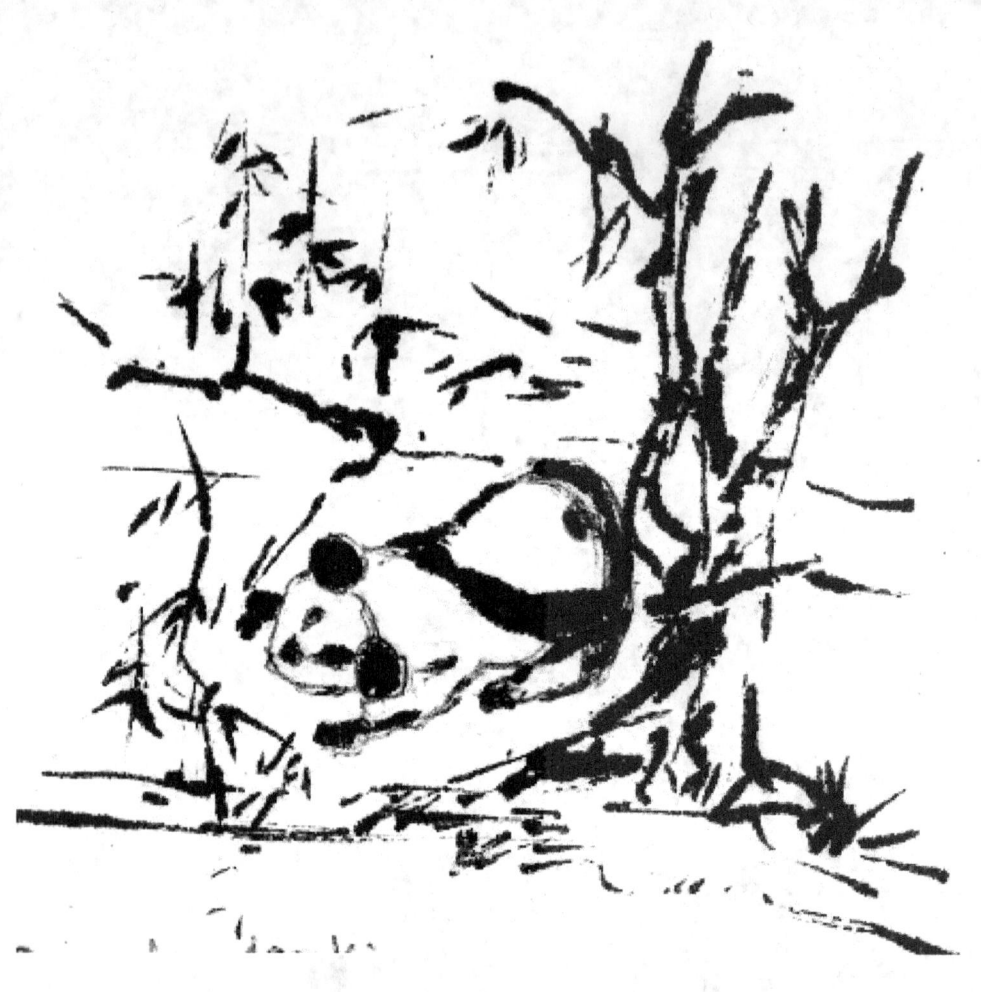

A panda takes a nap break after eating.

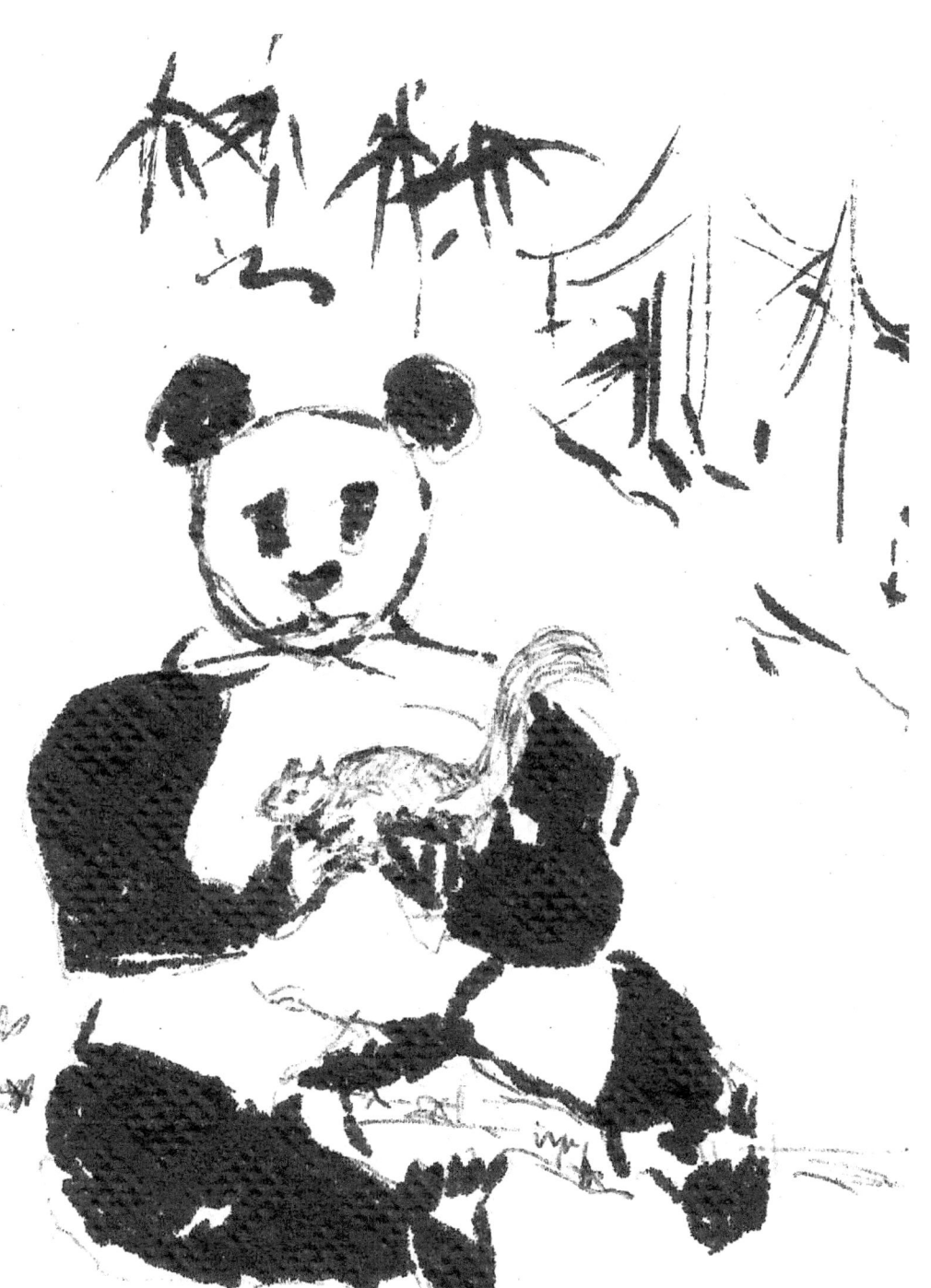

Vegan panda has a cute squirrel friend.

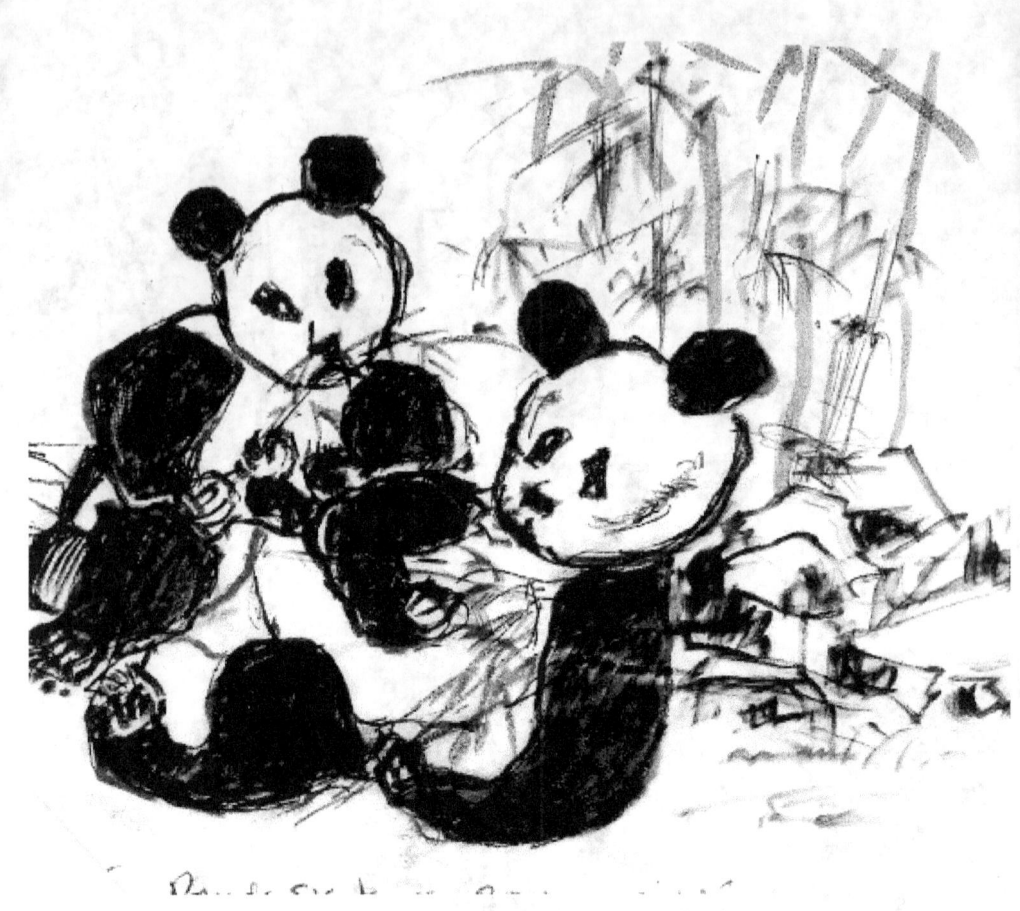

A panda couple rest after a sumptuous meal.

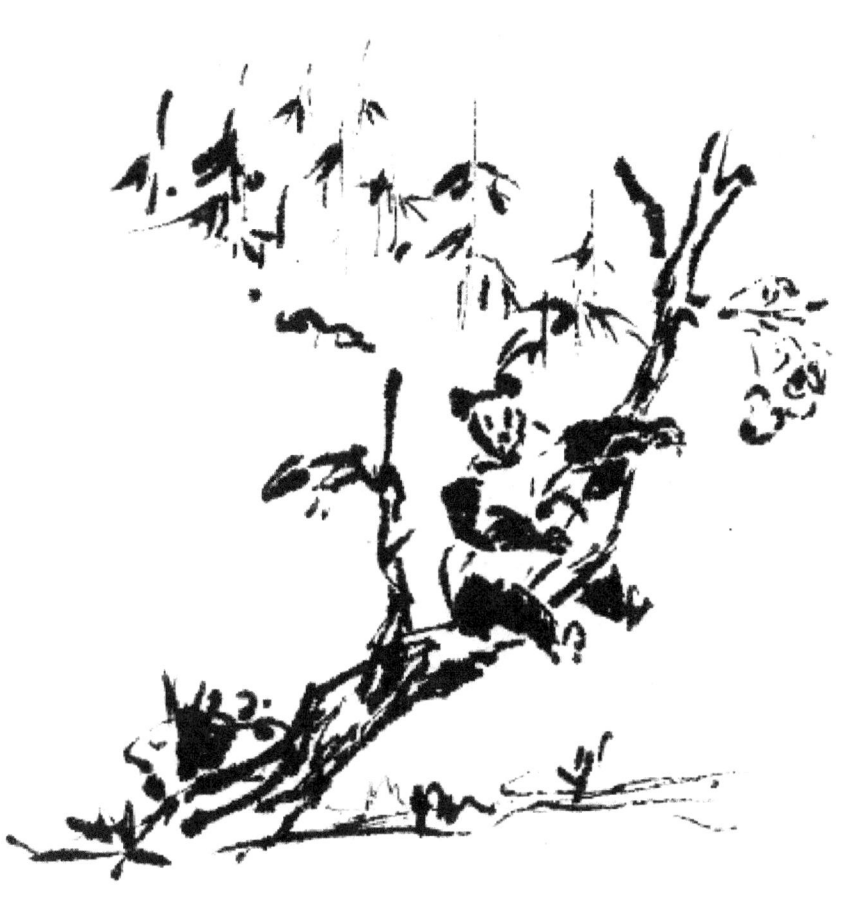

A panda climbs tree and reaches for delicious fruits.

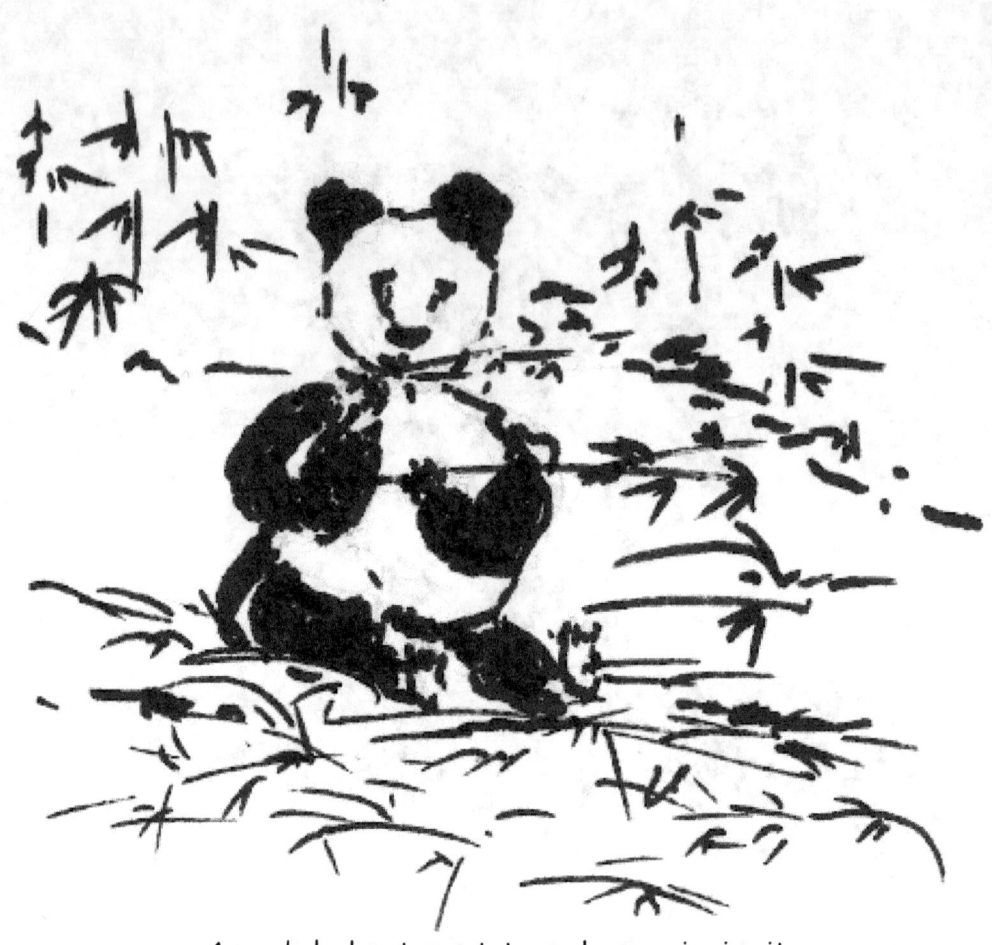

A panda looks at spectators who are viewing it.

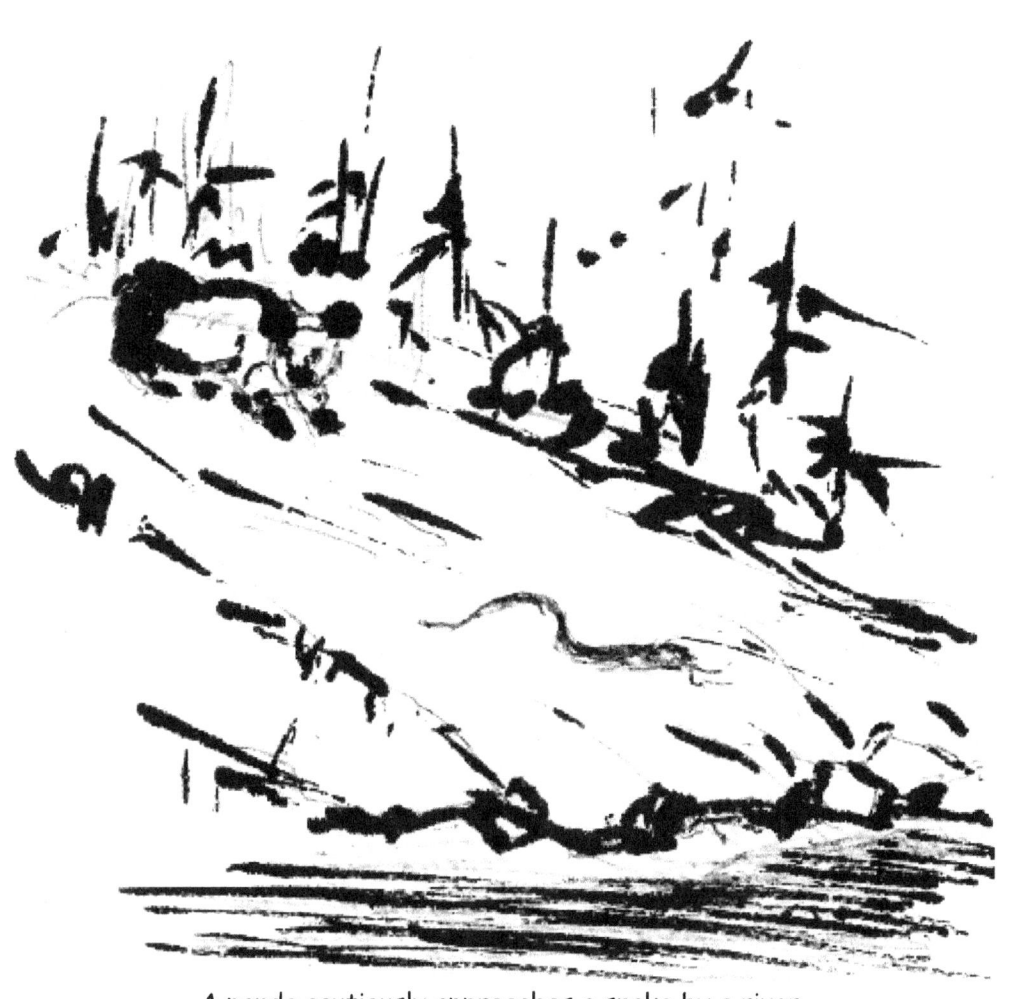

A panda cautiously approaches a snake by a river.

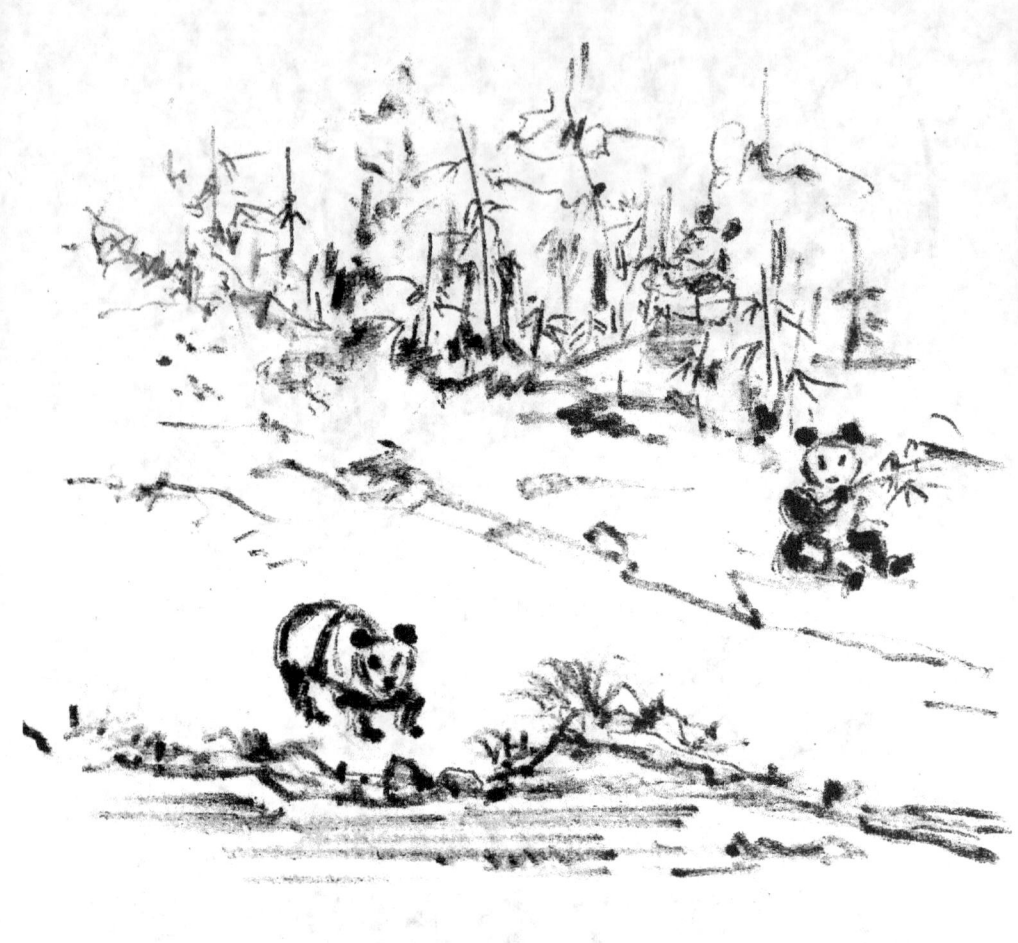

Pandas hide, eat and explore their natural habitat.

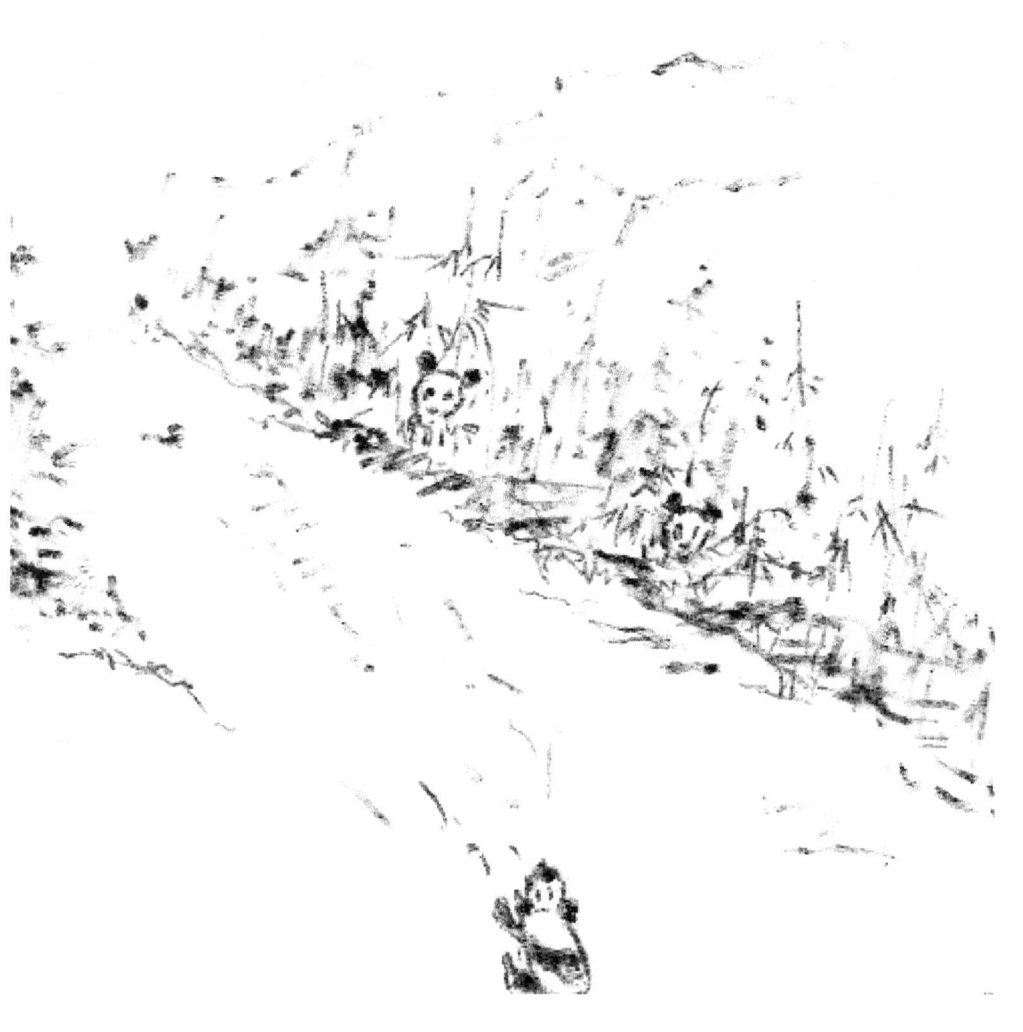

Young pandas play "hide and seek" in the bamboo cover.

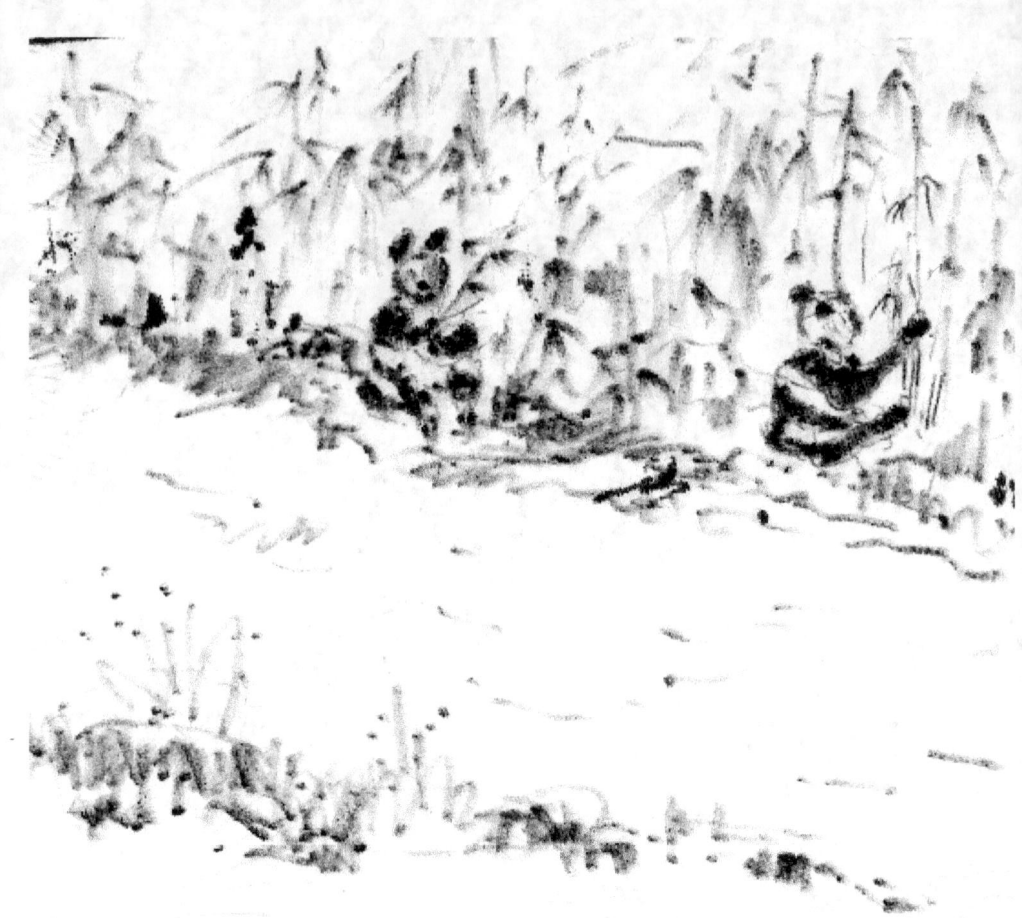

Pandas pick through the bamboo to find young tasty saplings.

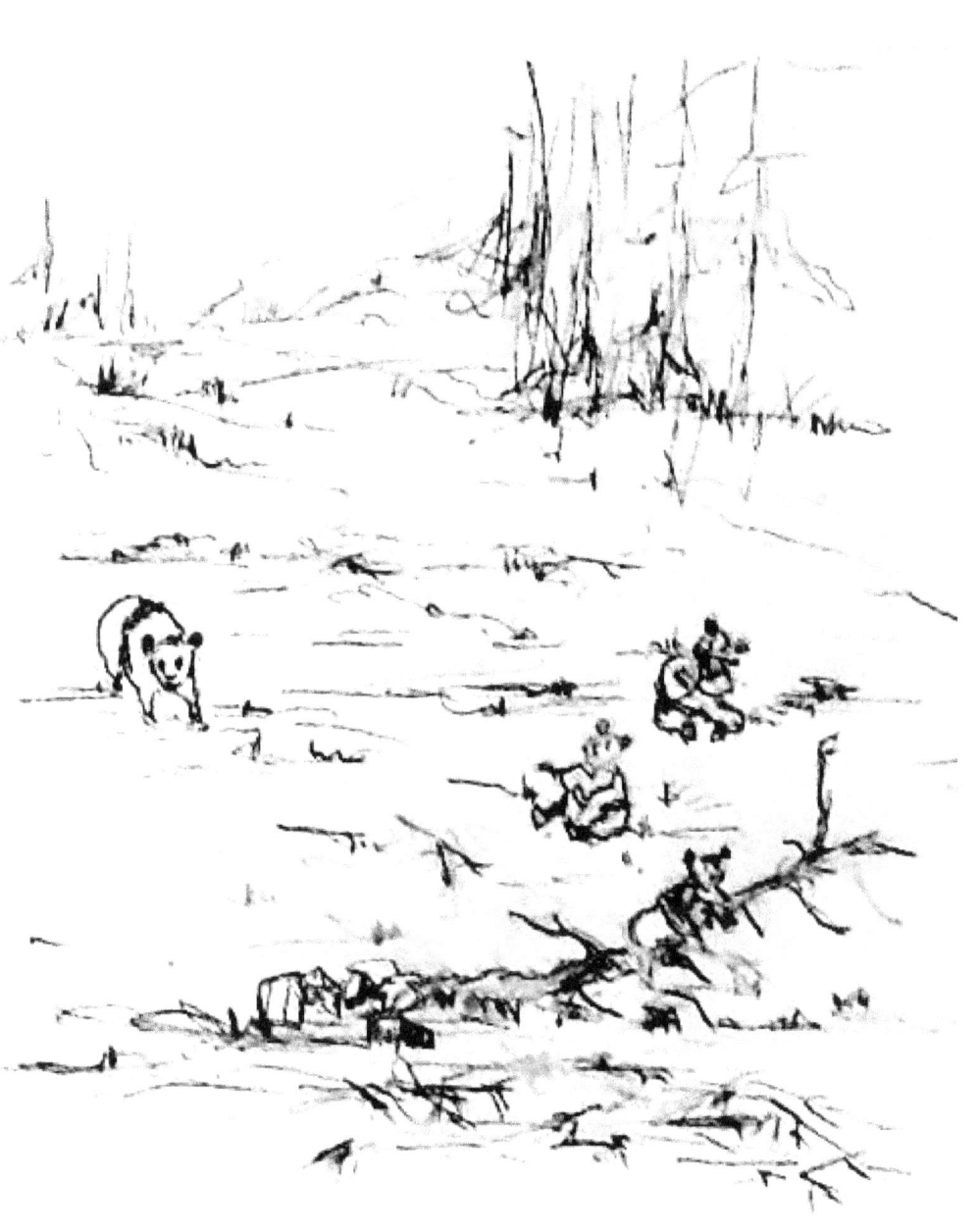

A panda family look for food in a deforested area.

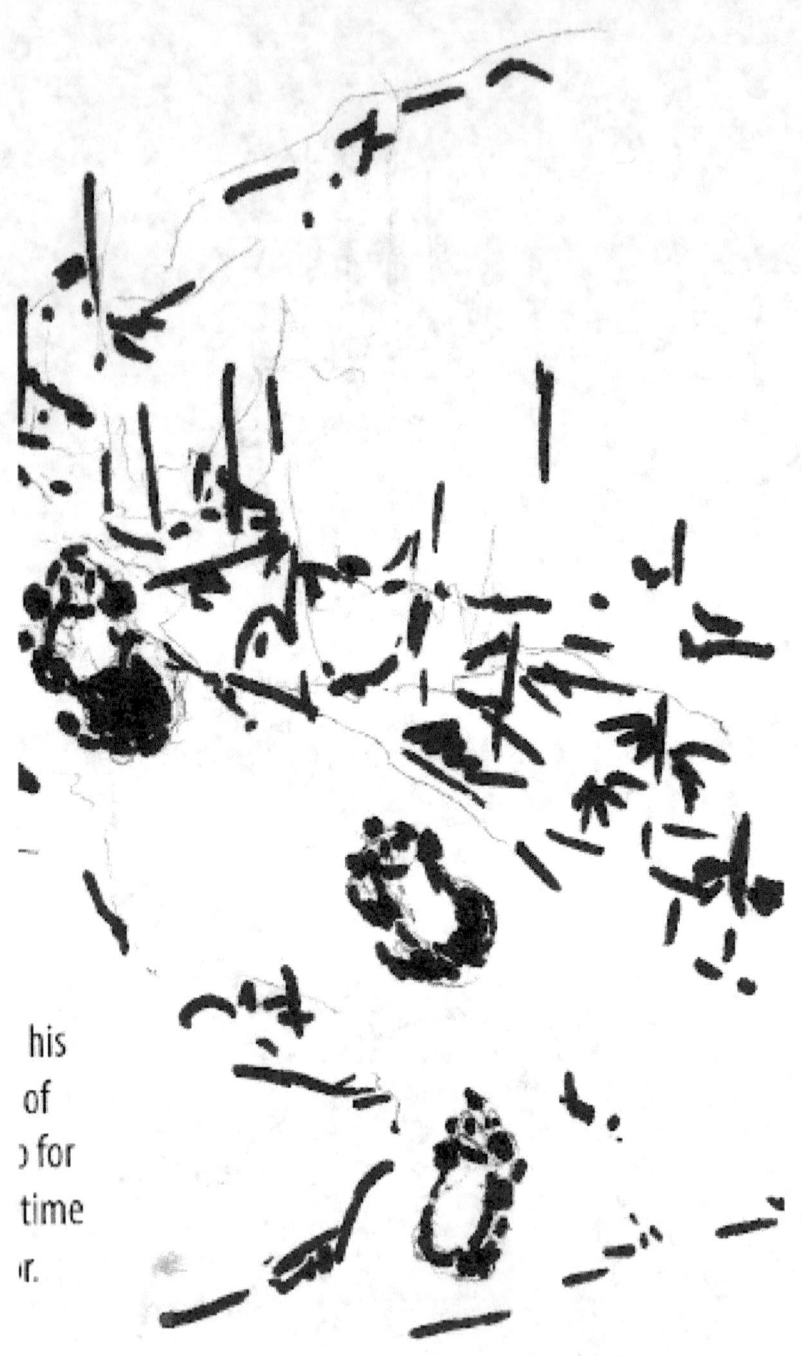

his
of
) for
time
r.

A panda family walk along a hiking trail.

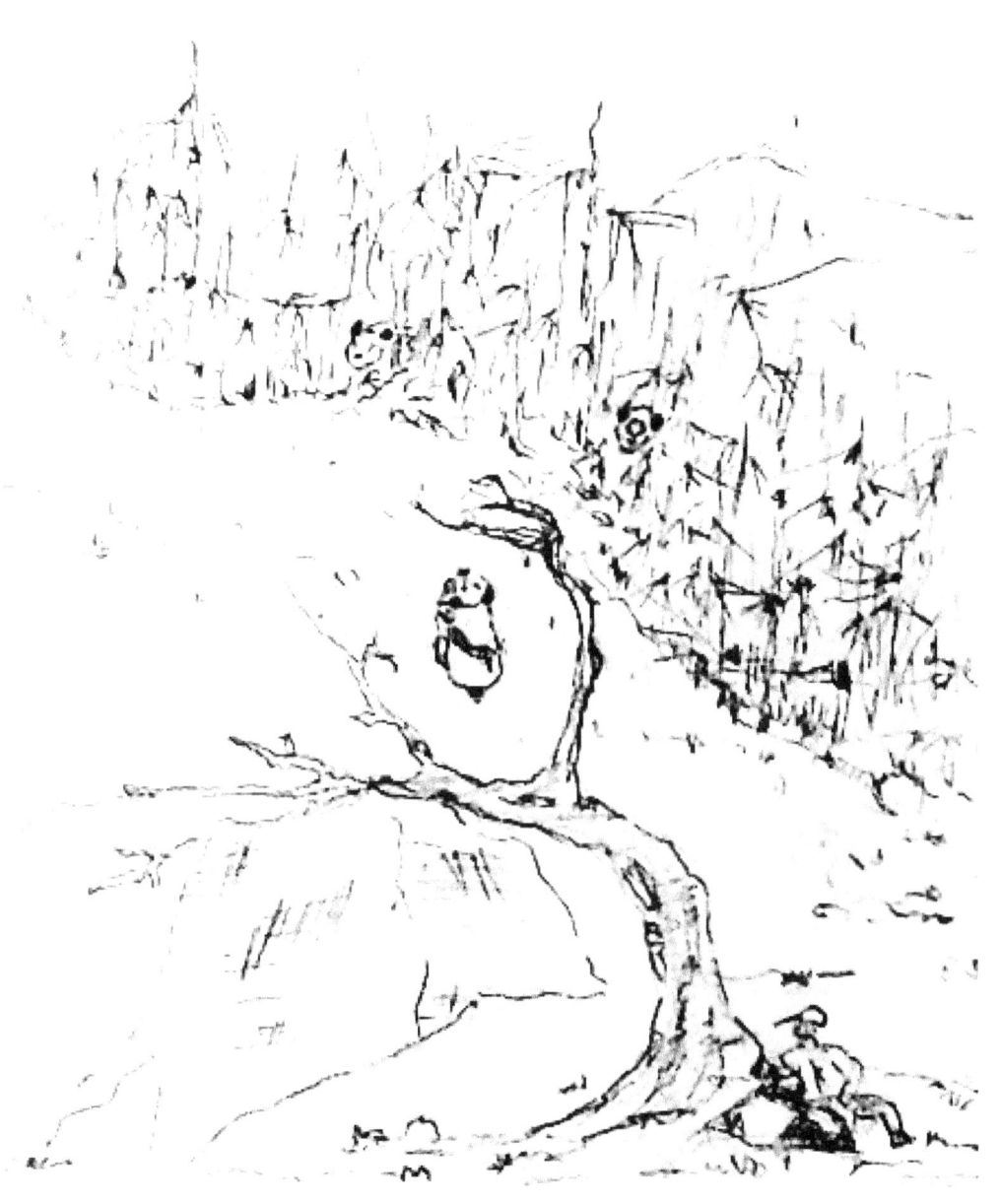

Pandas flee and hide from a pursuing poacher.

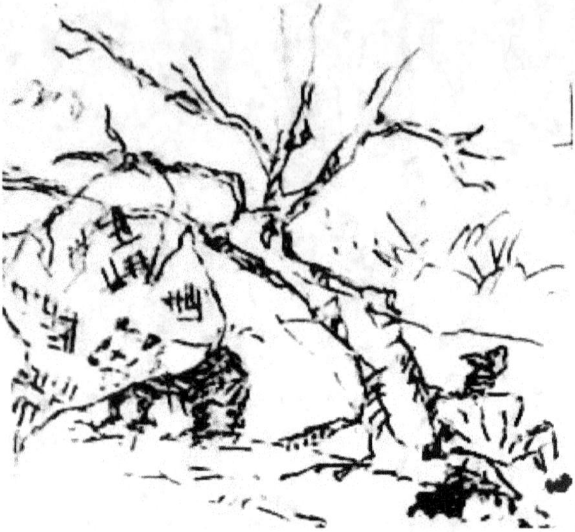

A panda drops a net on a panda. 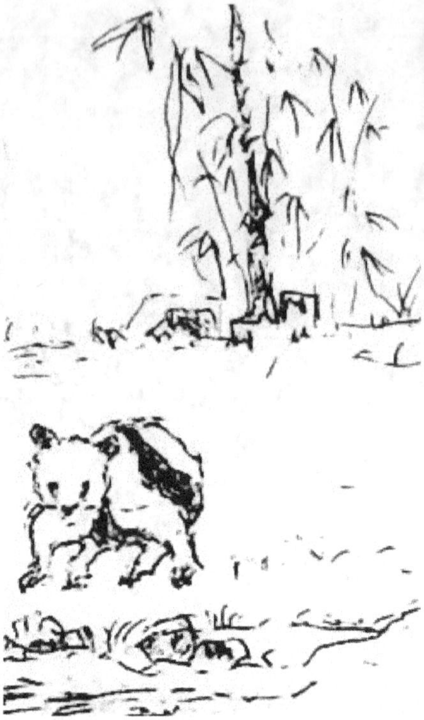
A panda flees from poacher.

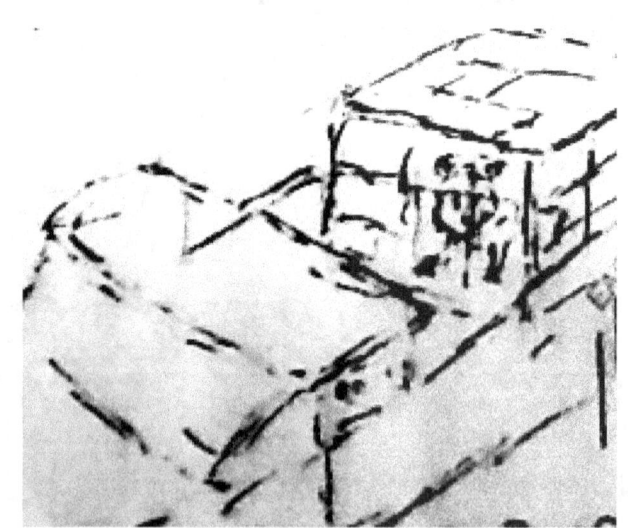

A captured panda sits in a cage on a poacher's truck.

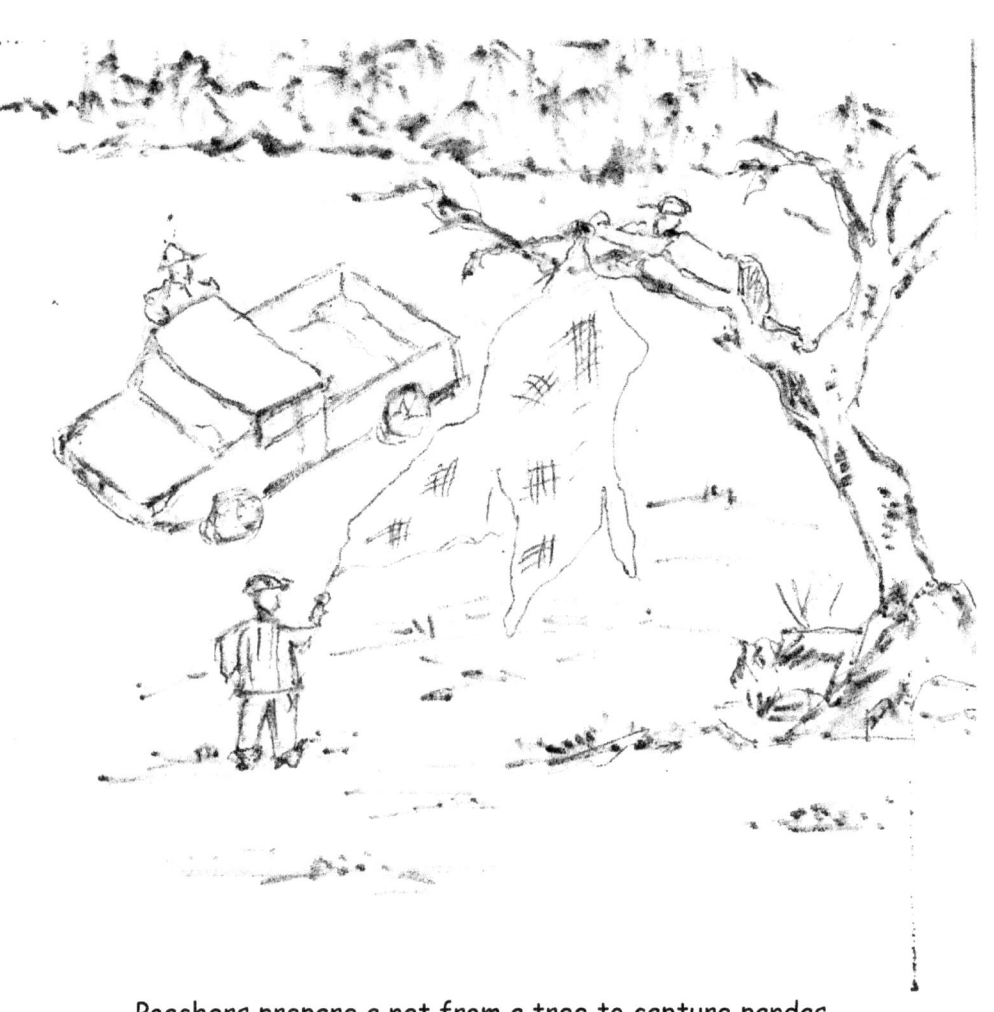

Poachers prepare a net from a tree to capture pandas.

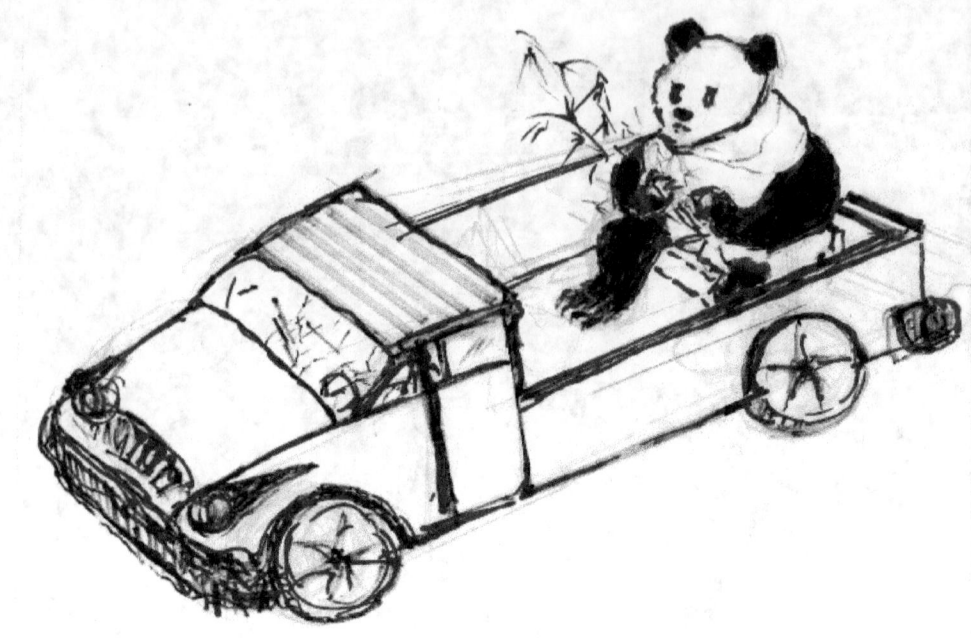

A captured panda is taken away in a poacher's truck.

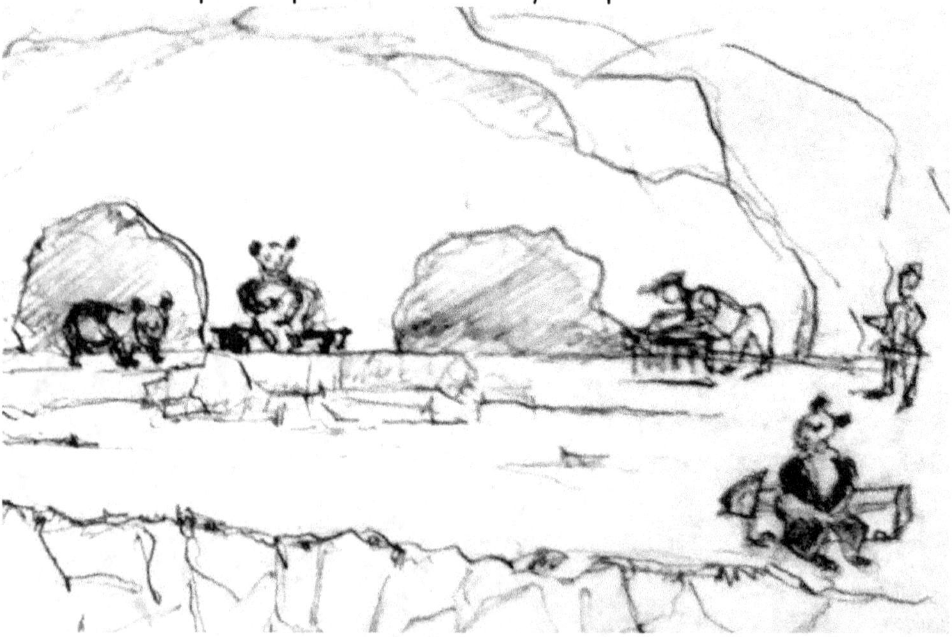

Zoo keepers feeding pandas in captivity.

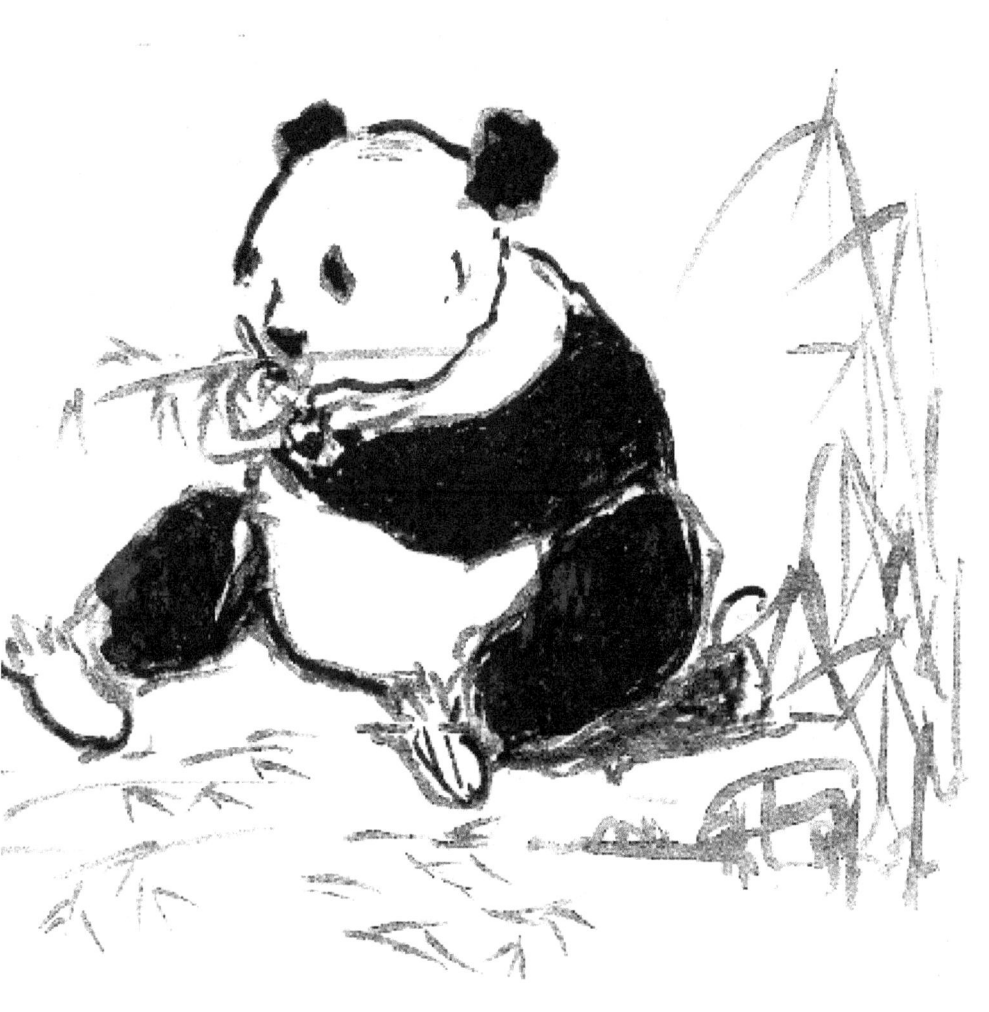

A panda savoring sweet young bamboo leaves.

A panda rolling on its back.

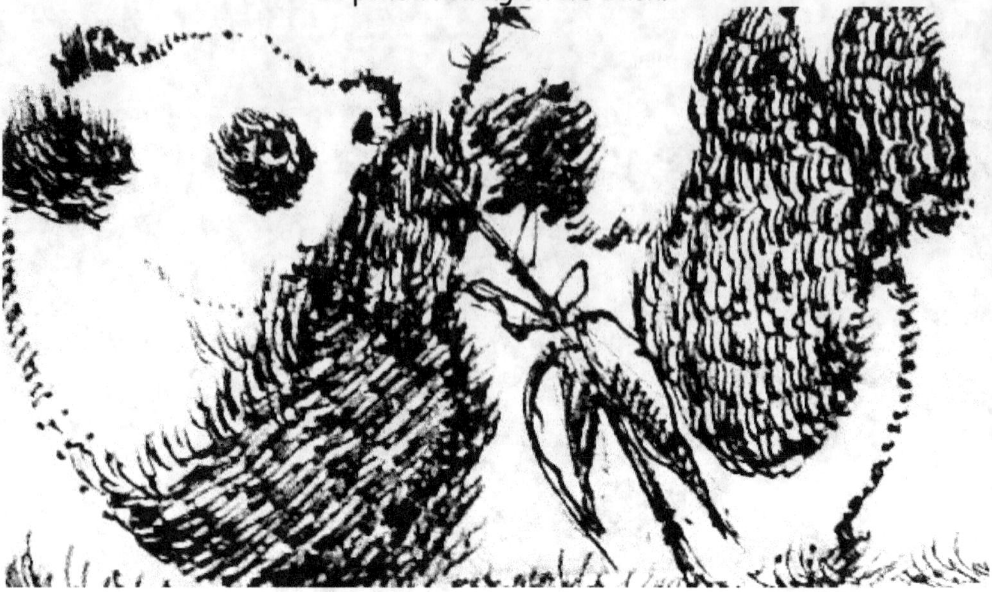

Pandas sitting in a zoo, watching people look at them.

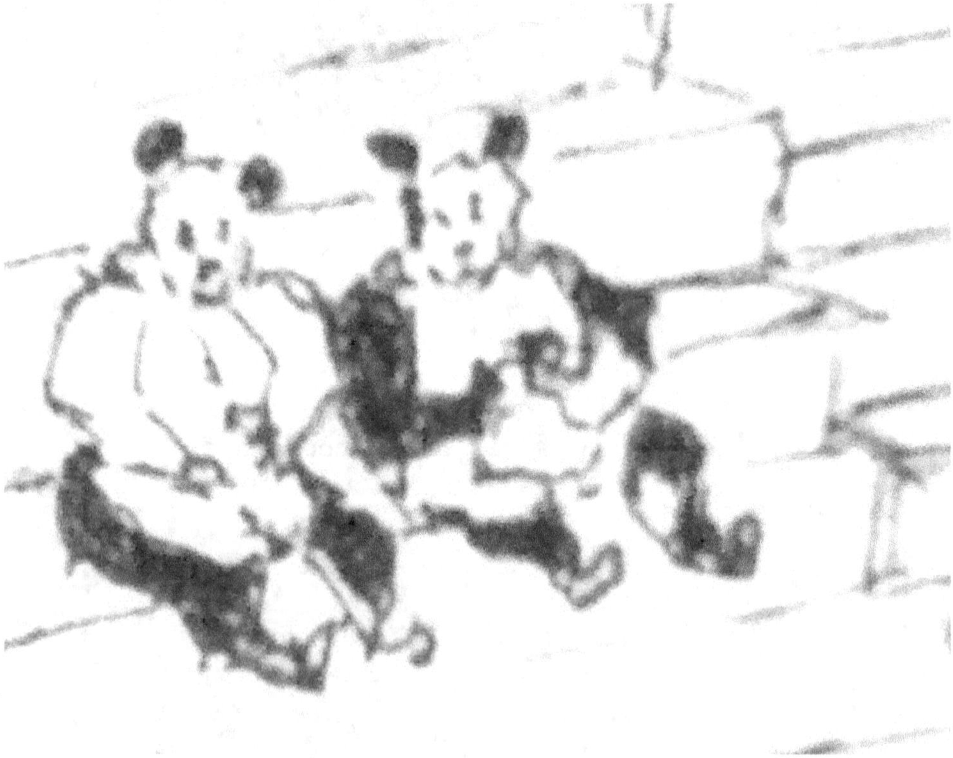

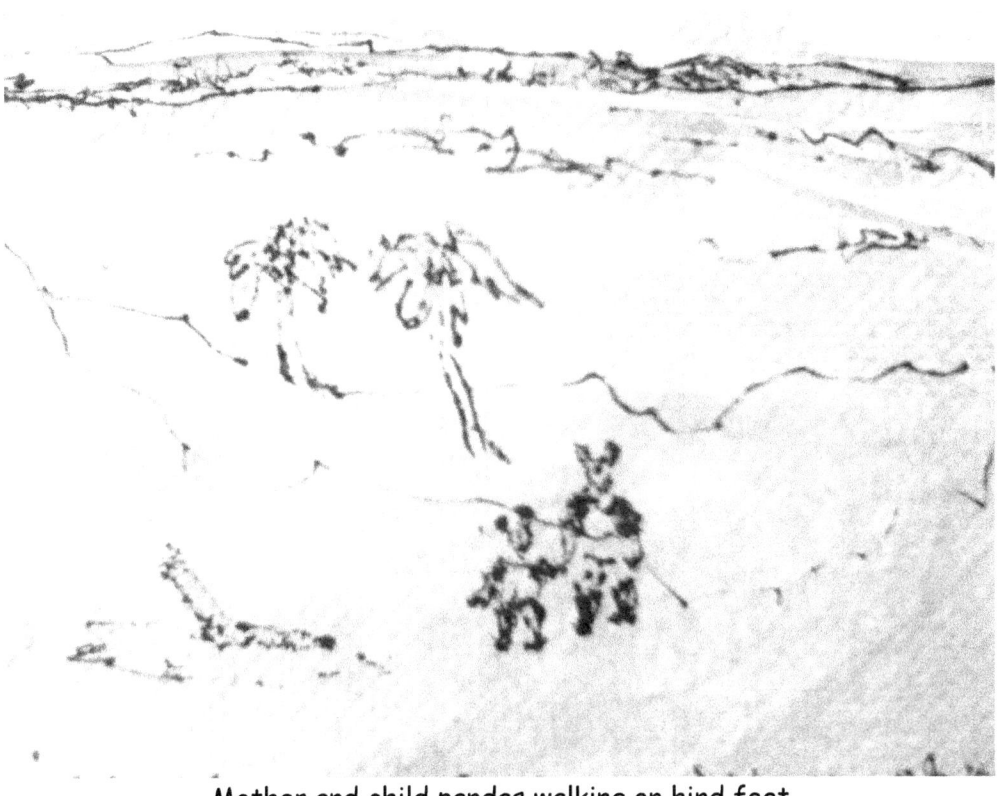

Mother and child pandas walking on hind feet

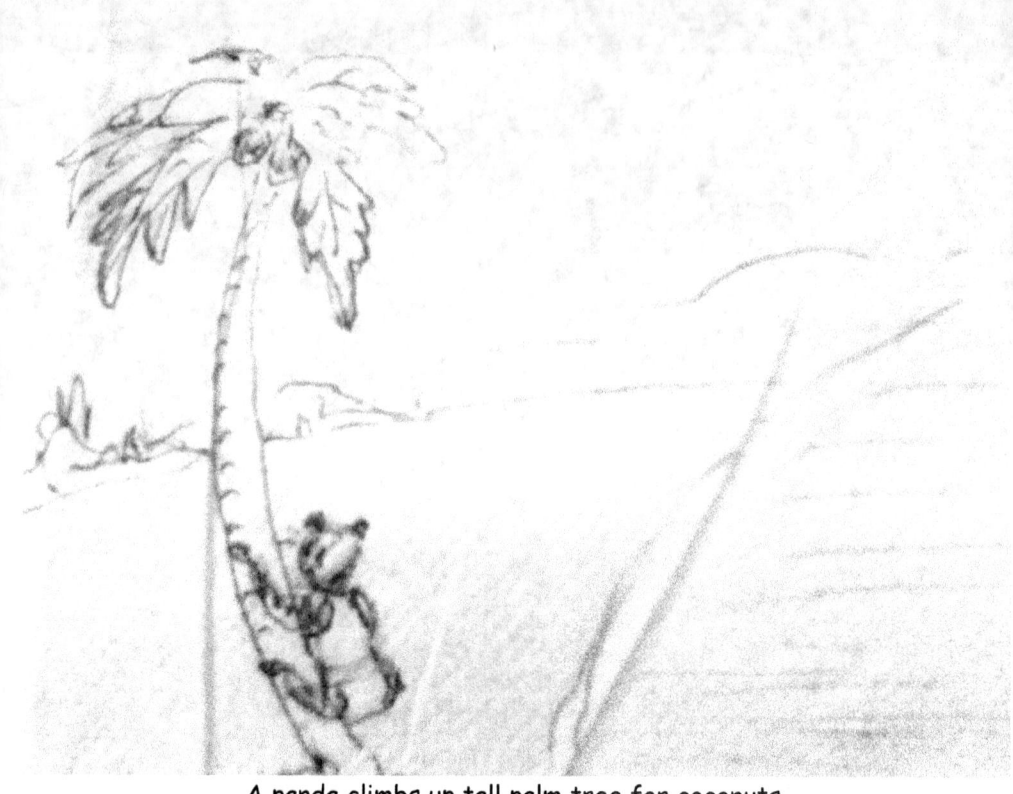

A panda climbs up tall palm tree for coconuts.

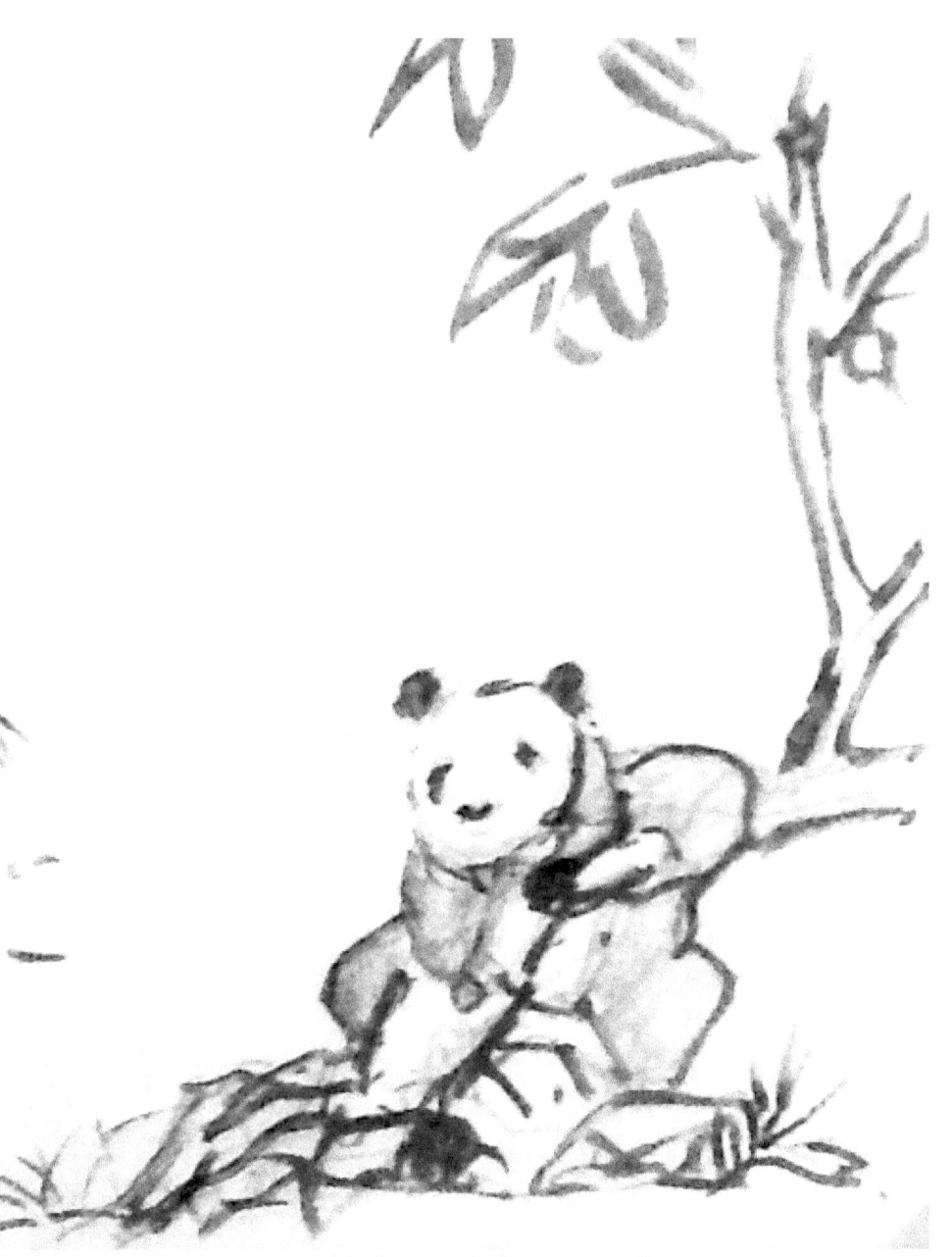

A scared baby panda hugs a small tree.

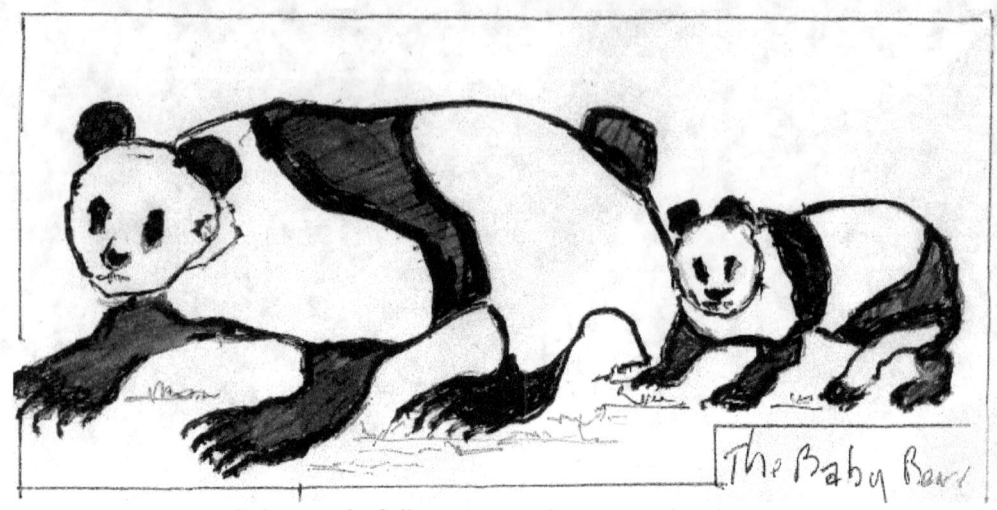

Baby panda follows its mother very closely.

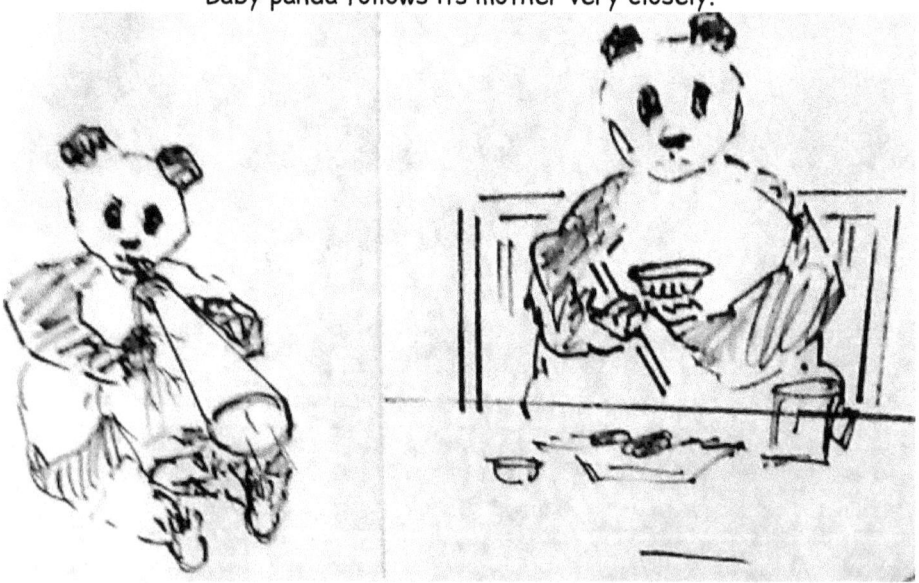

Teen panda plays horn while its mother makes a Chinese food veggie dinner.

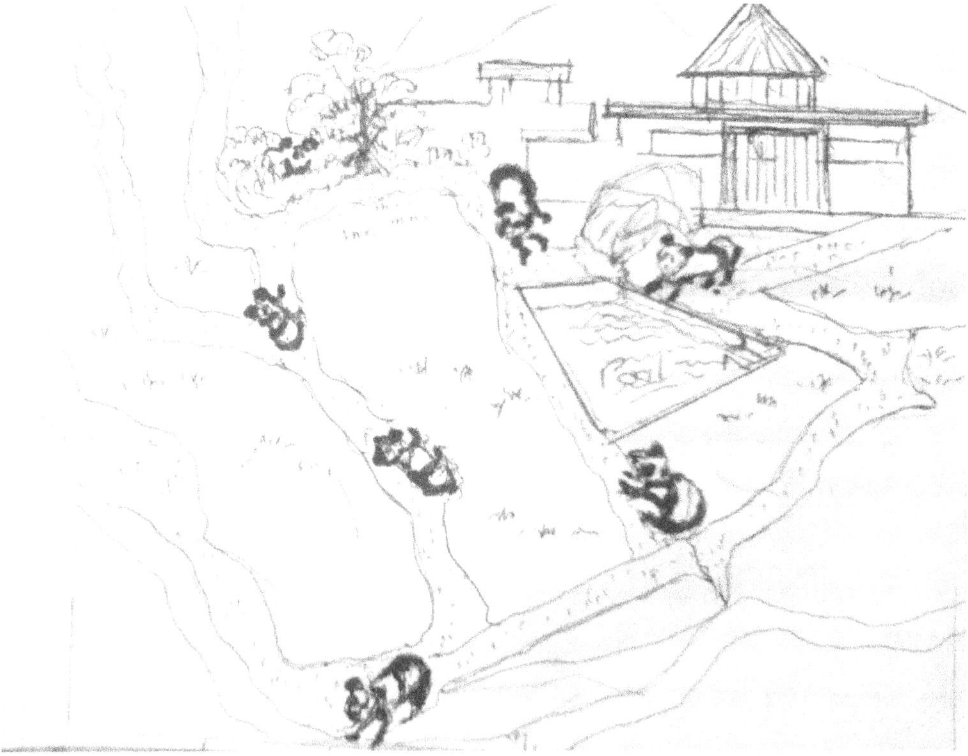

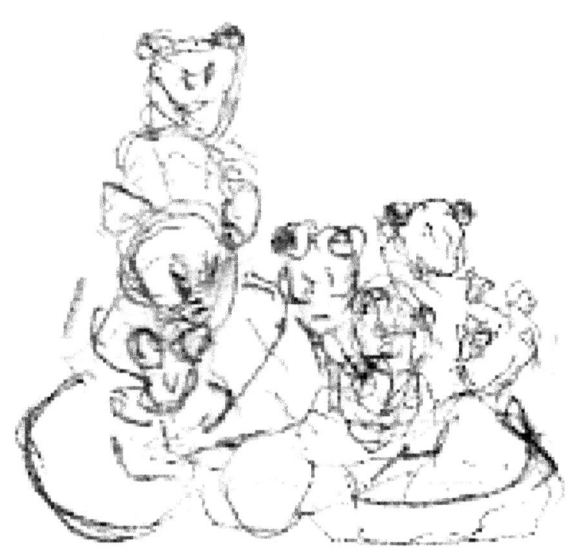

Pandas look for veggies in a backyard garden, but not much was growing.

Pandas at zoo looking back at people.

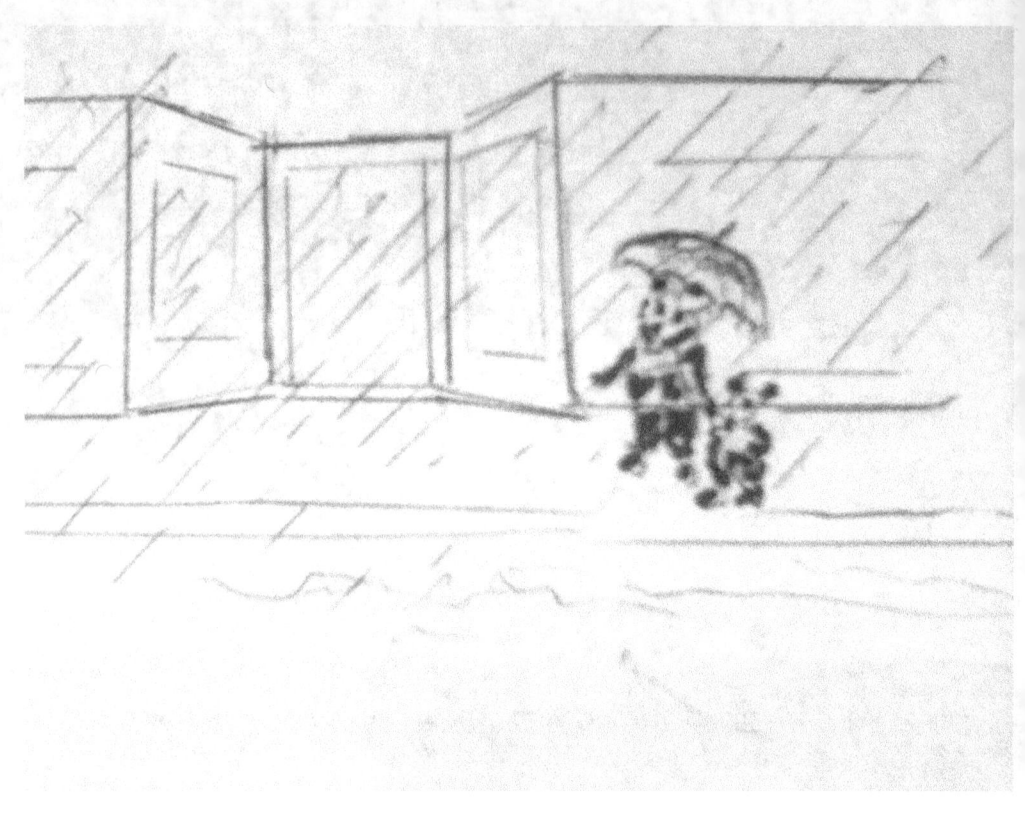

Mother panda and her cub enjoy walking in the rain.

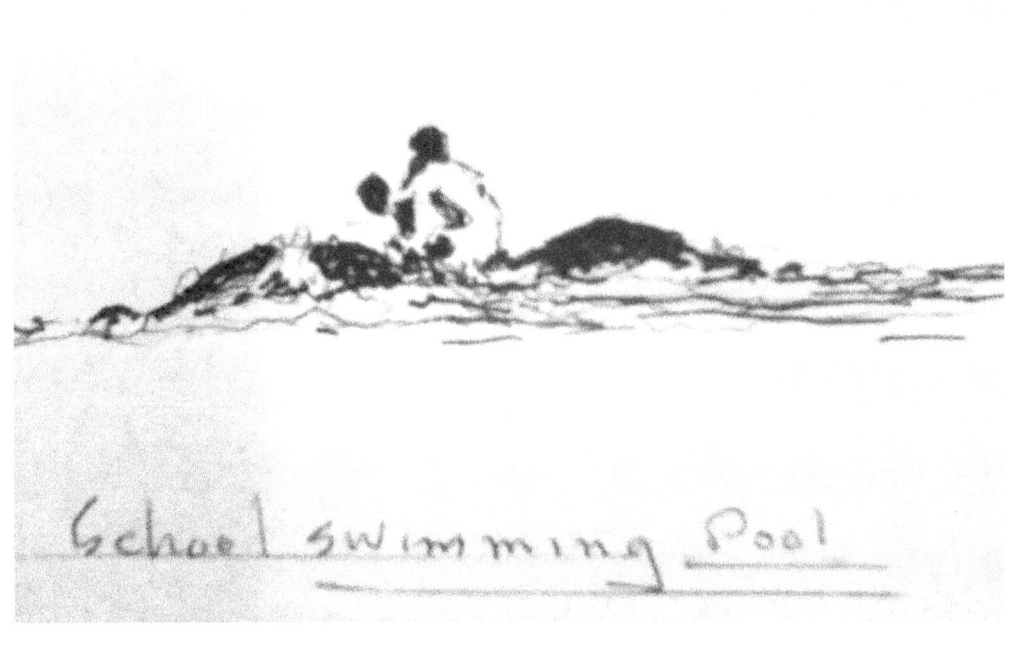

A teen panda swims in the high school pool on a very hot day.

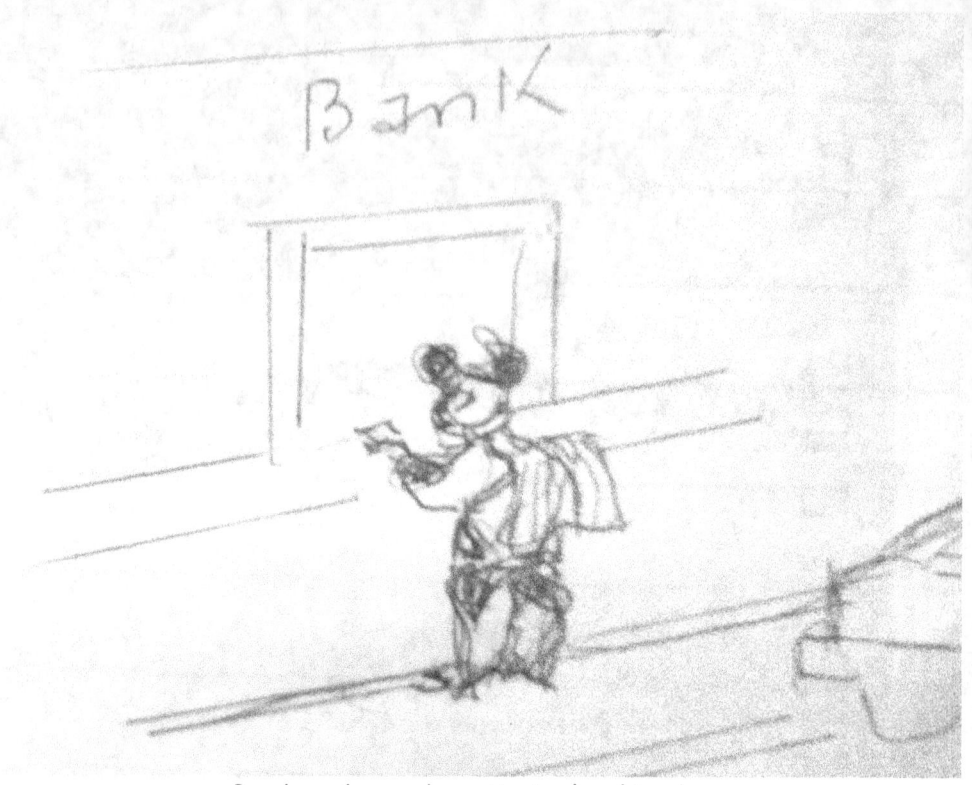

Panda makes a deposit at a local bank.

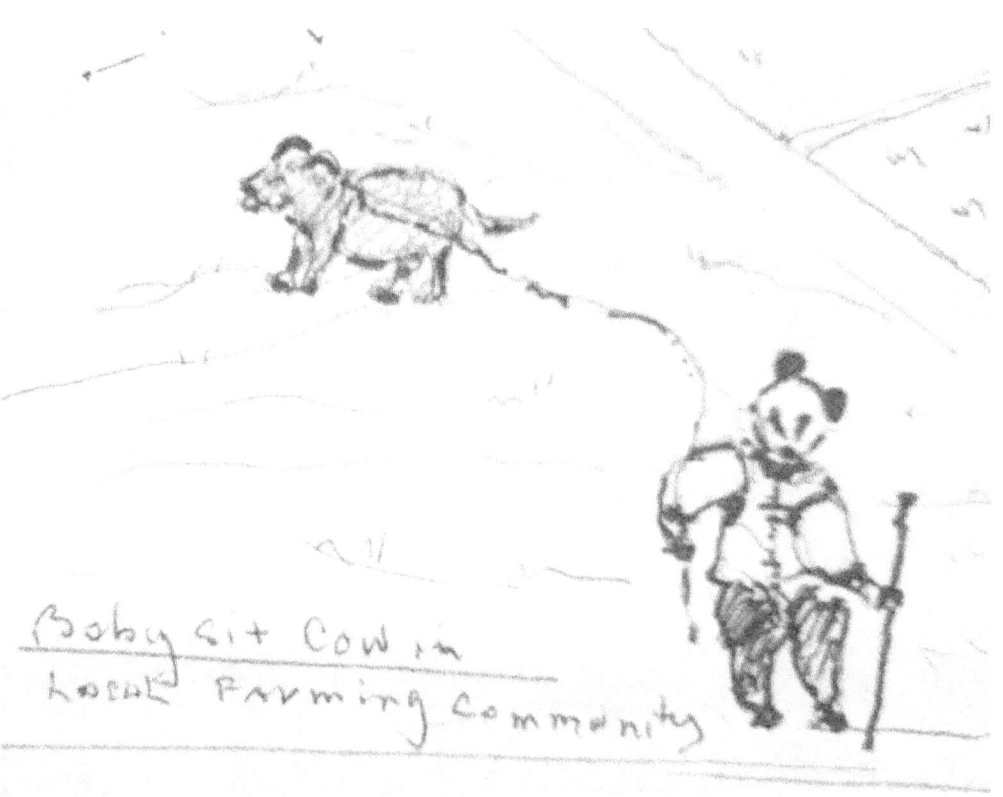

Panda walks his dog, thinking it's a calf.

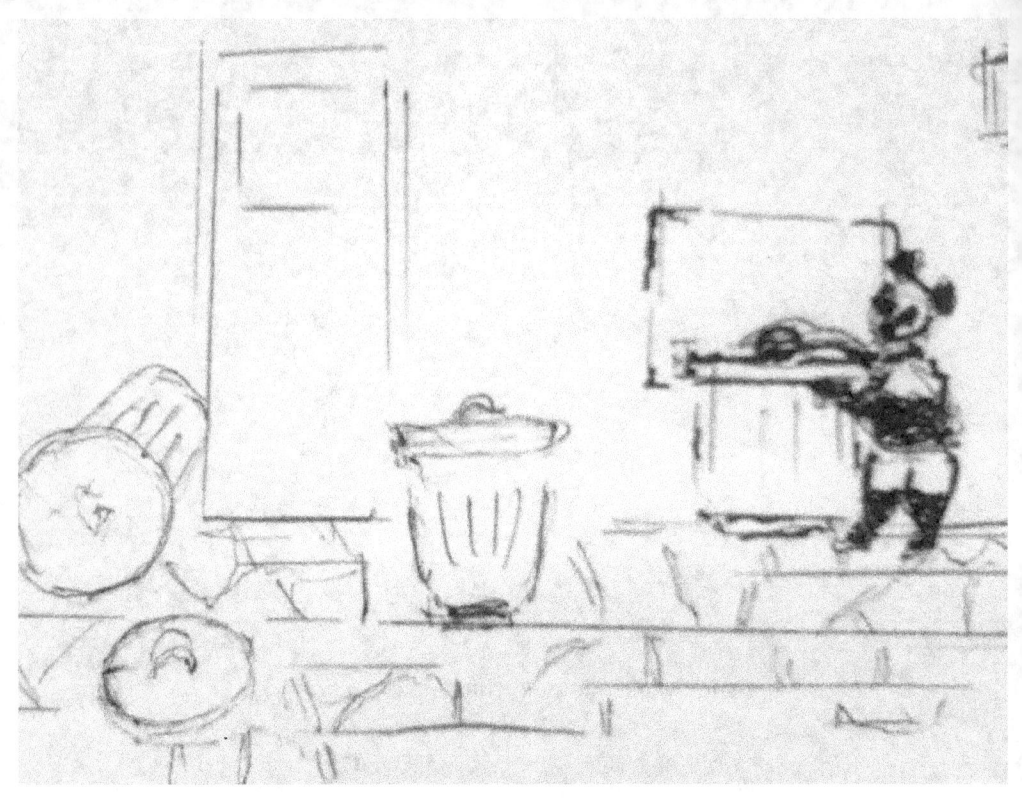

A panda knocks over garbage cans while looking for food.

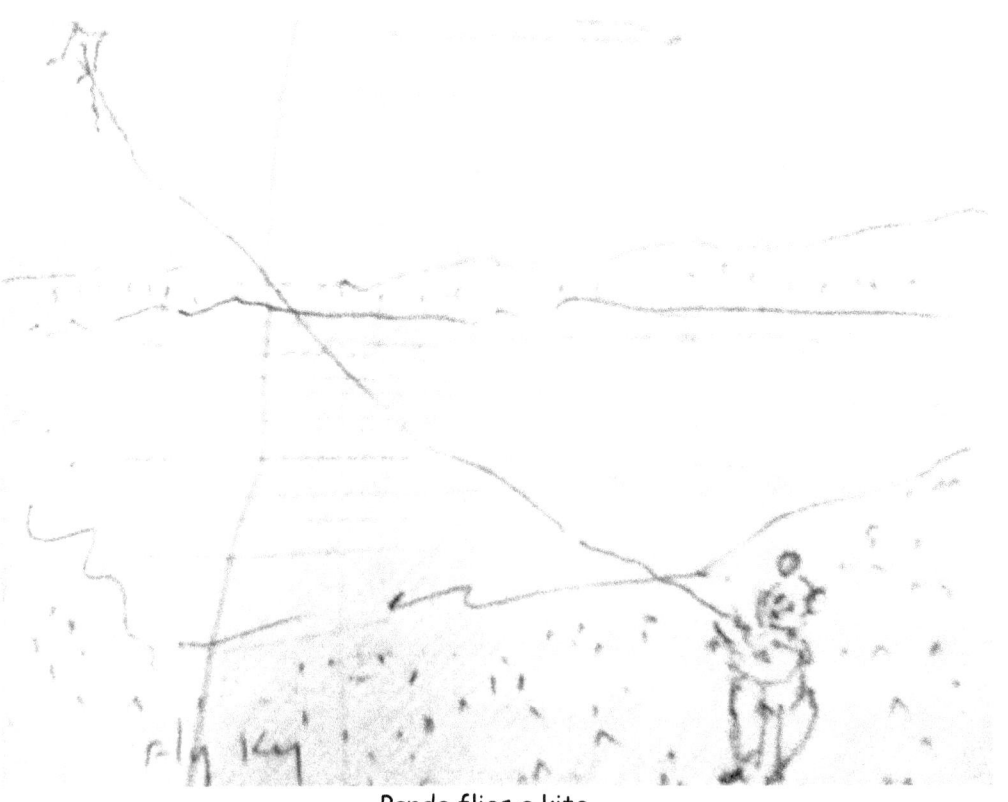

Panda flies a kite.

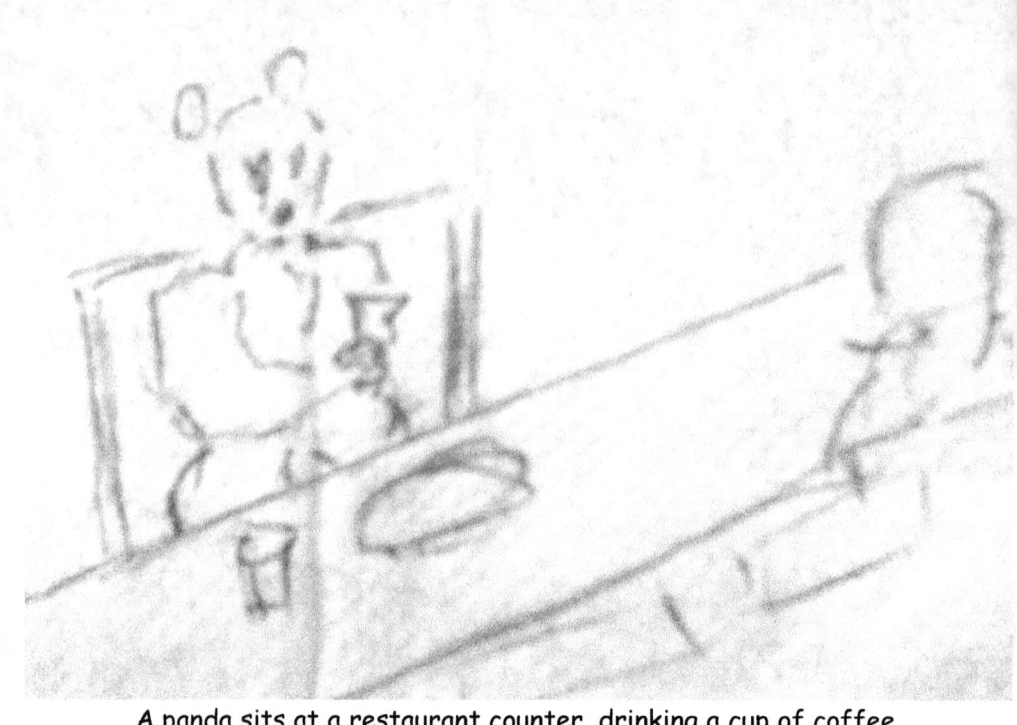

A panda sits at a restaurant counter, drinking a cup of coffee.

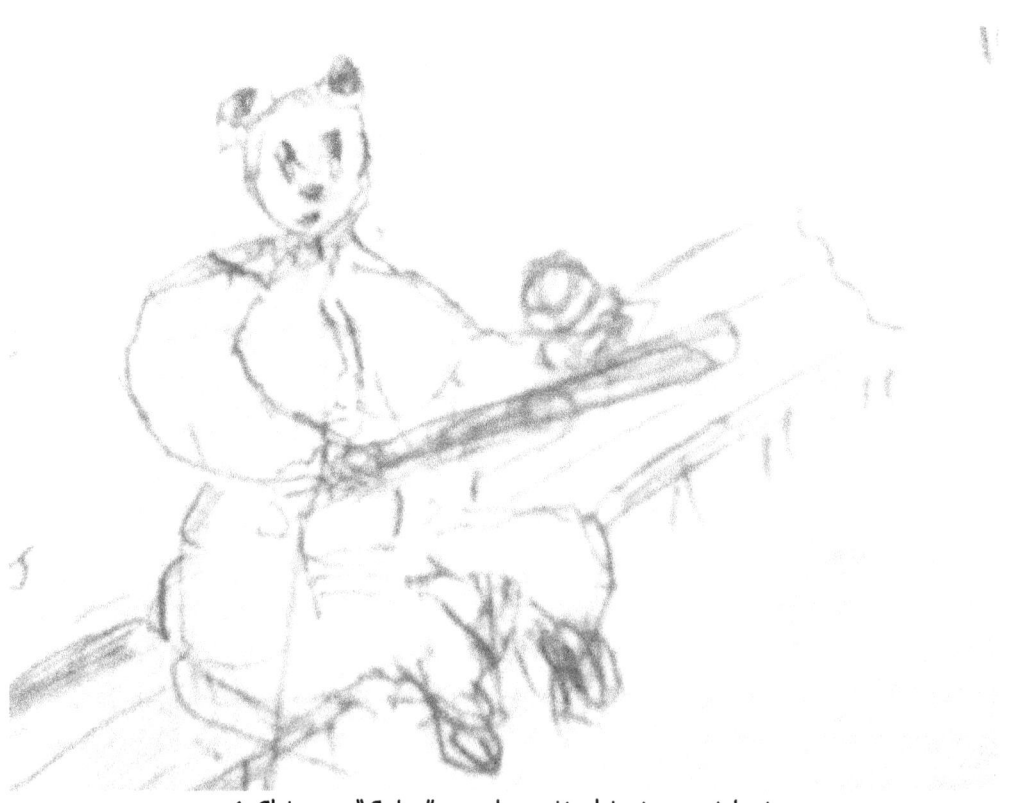

A Chicago "Cubs" panda waits his turn at bat.

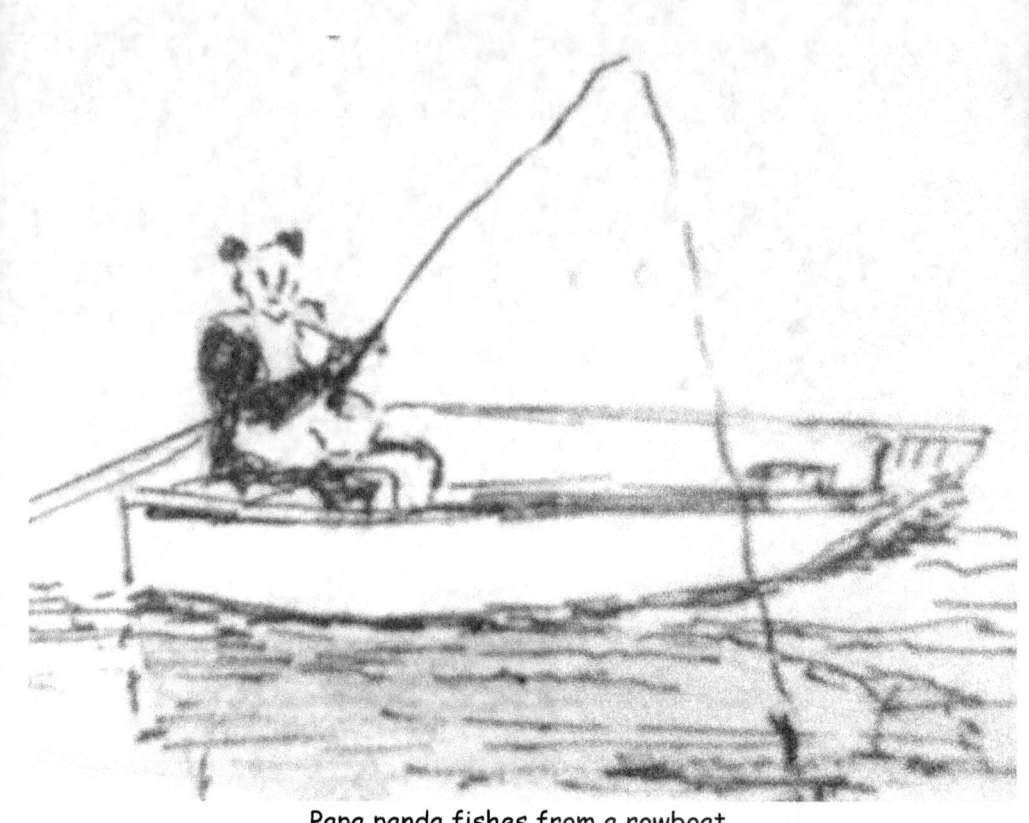

Papa panda fishes from a rowboat.

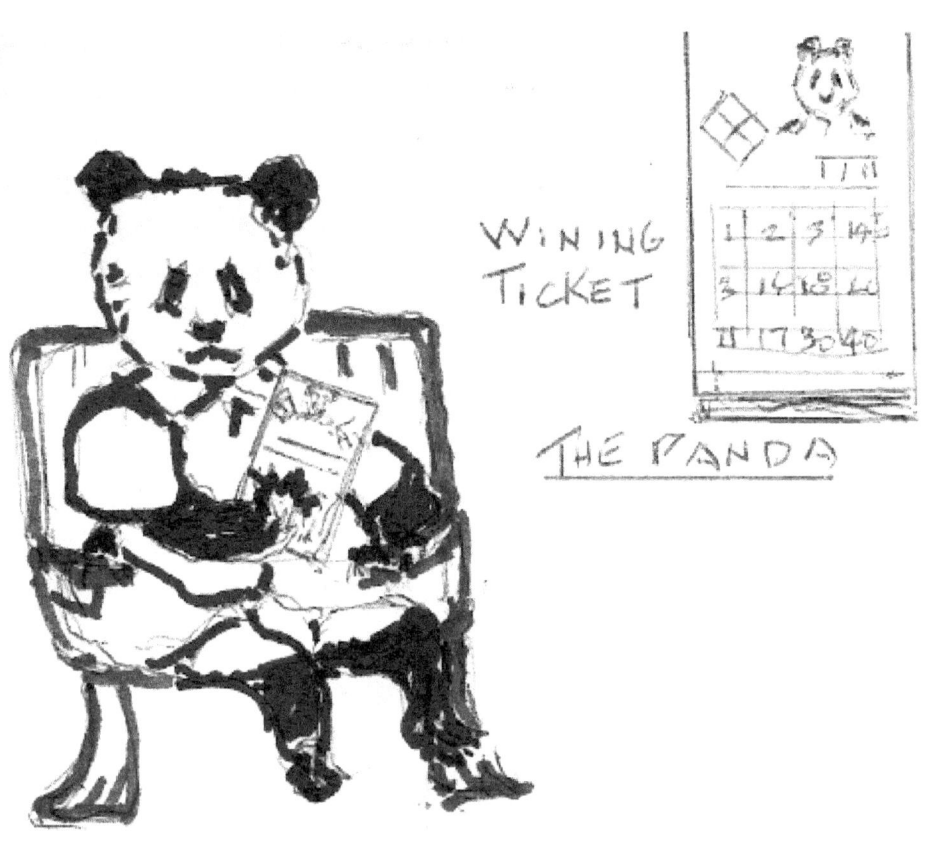

Mama panda plays the Power Ball lottery. Will she win?

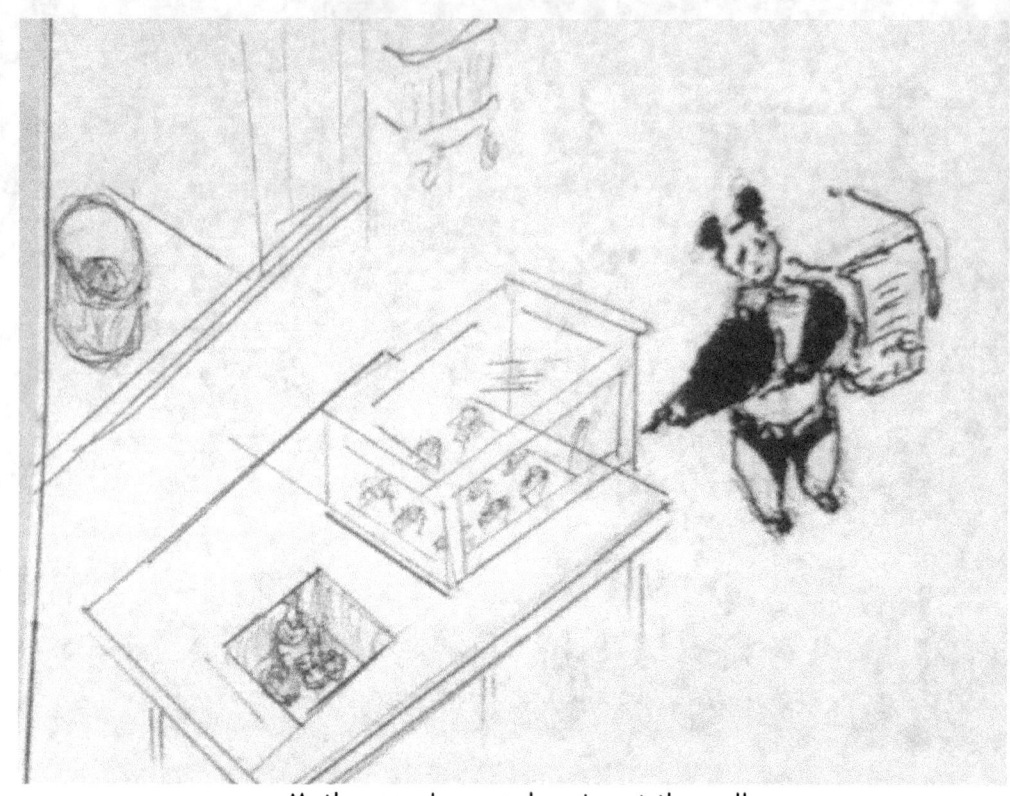

Mother panda goes shopping at the mall.

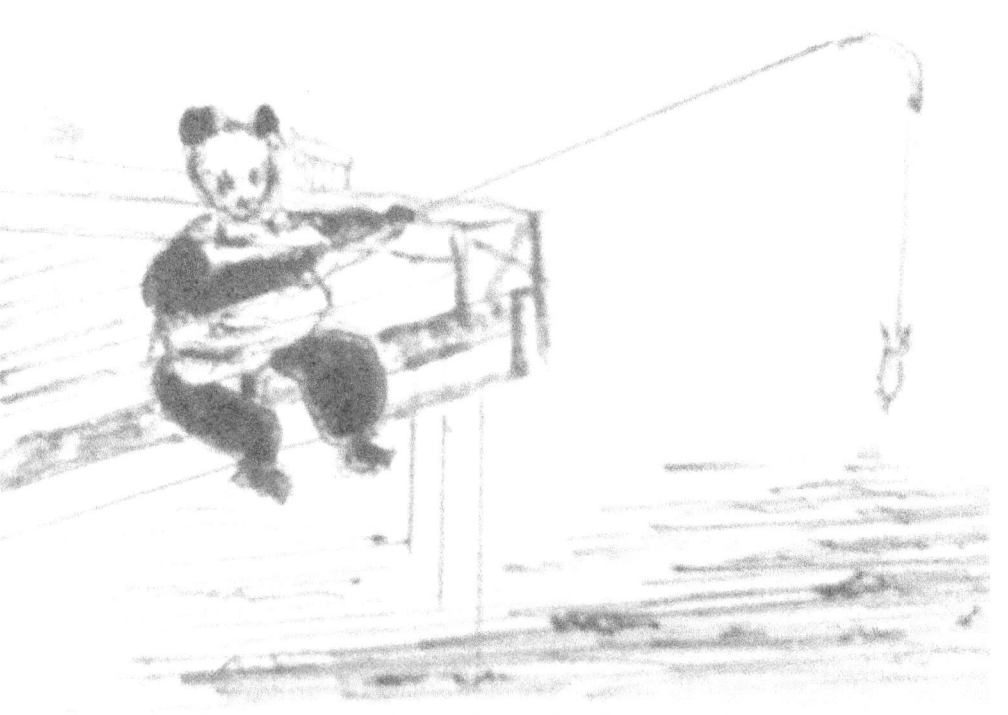

Big brother panda catches a fish from the dock.

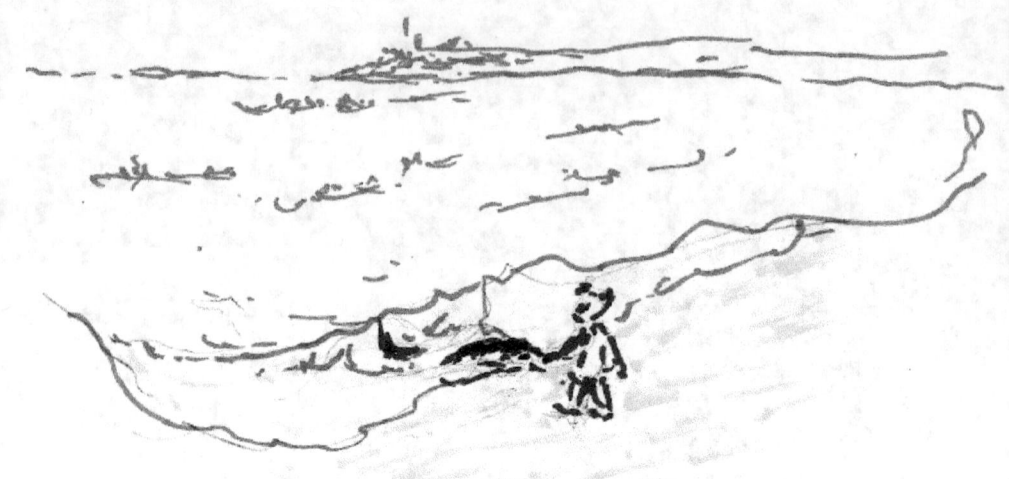

Panda child watches waves roll in at the beach. Will he get wet?

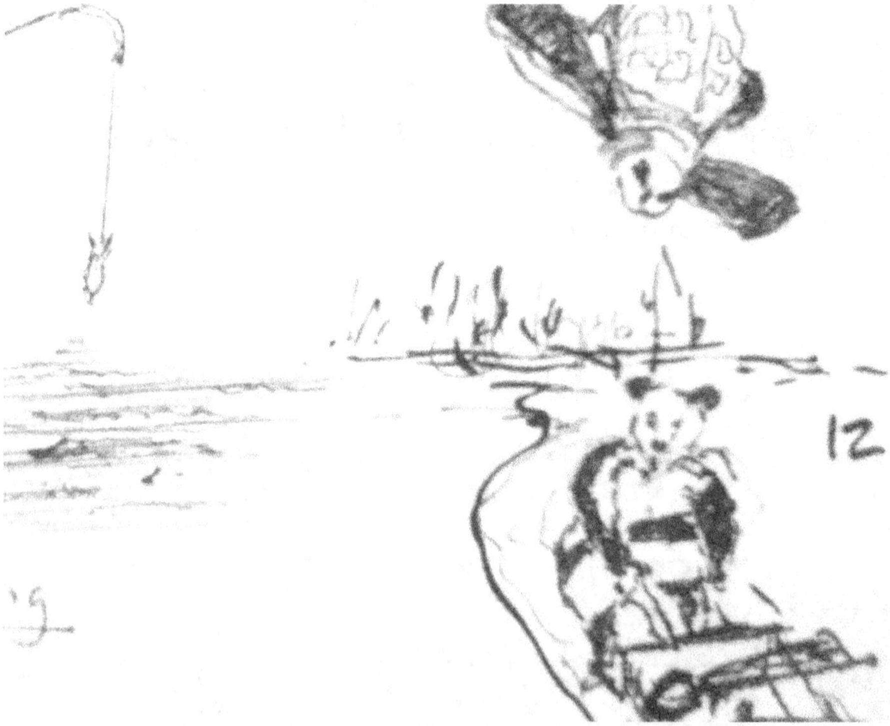

Sister panda races a flying turtle on her Sea Do.

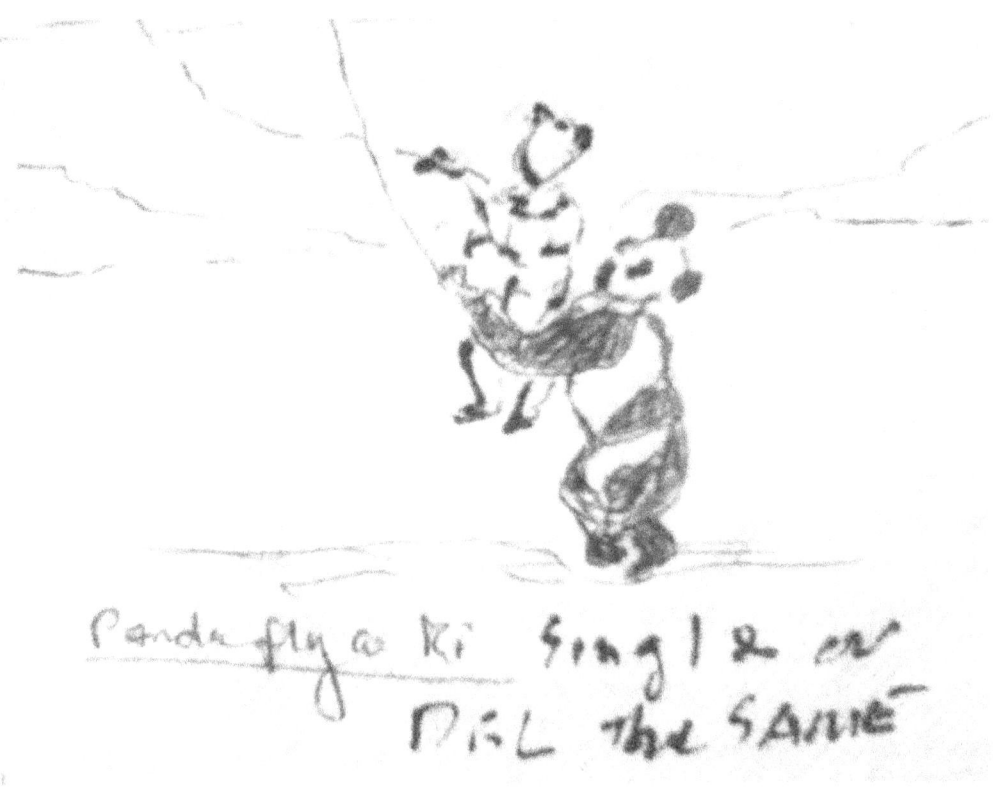

Panda fly a ki Singl a on
DiL the SAME

Brother and sister pandas fly kites together.

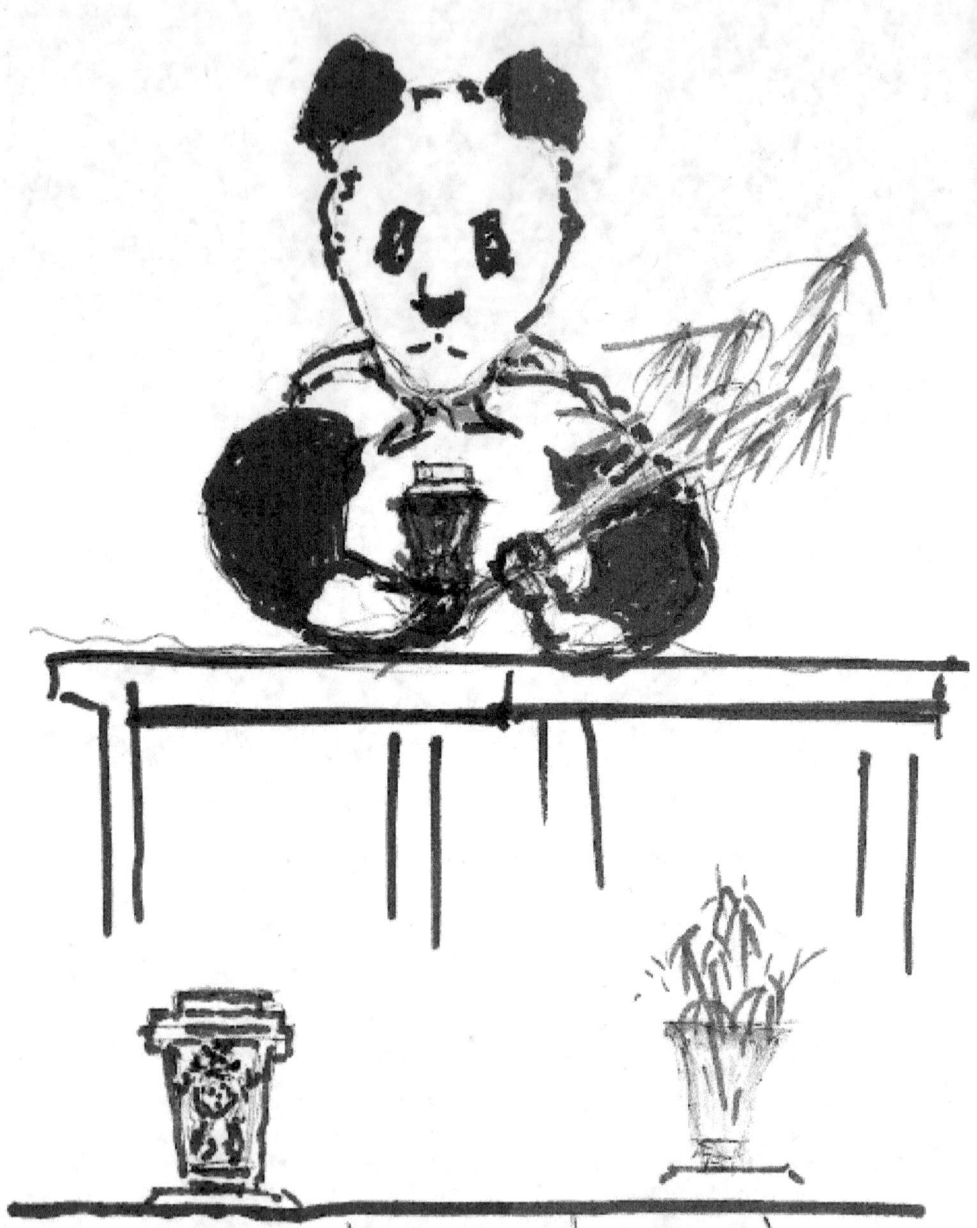

Panda drinks java and munches on bamboo.

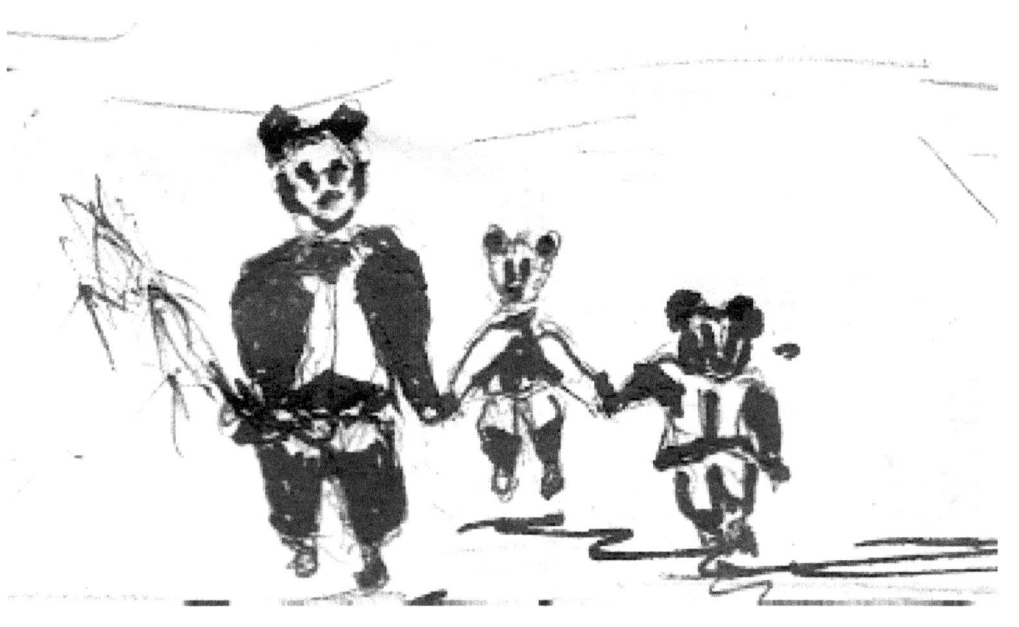

Daddy panda walks his cubs to school.

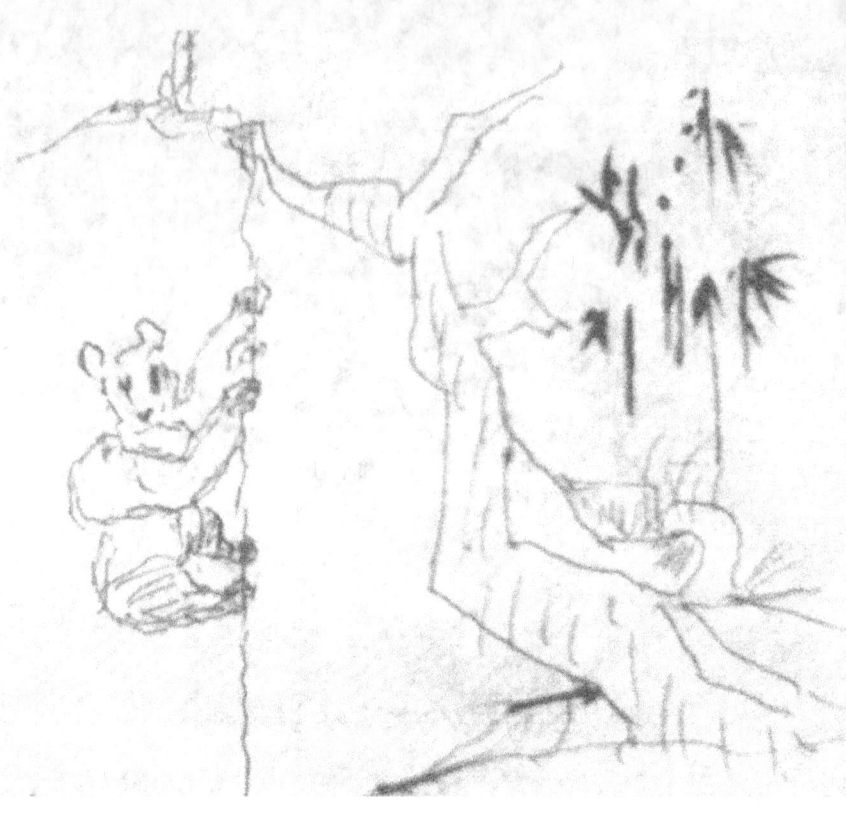

Daring panda climbs up rope to a very tall tree.

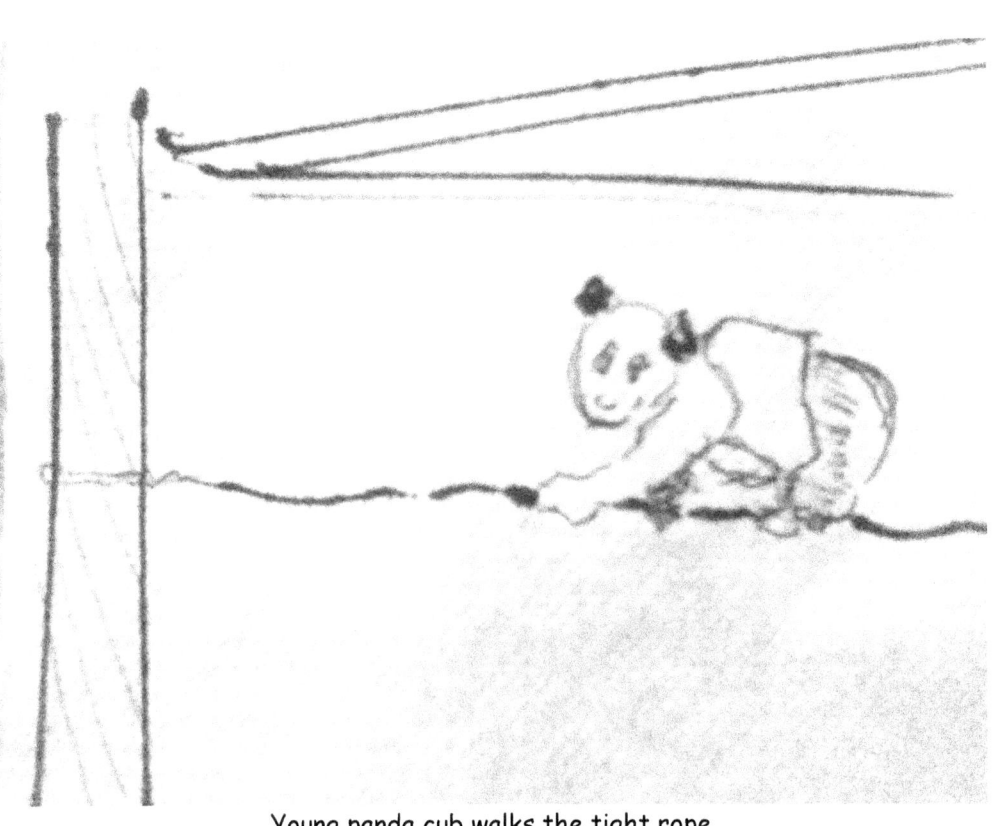

Young panda cub walks the tight rope.

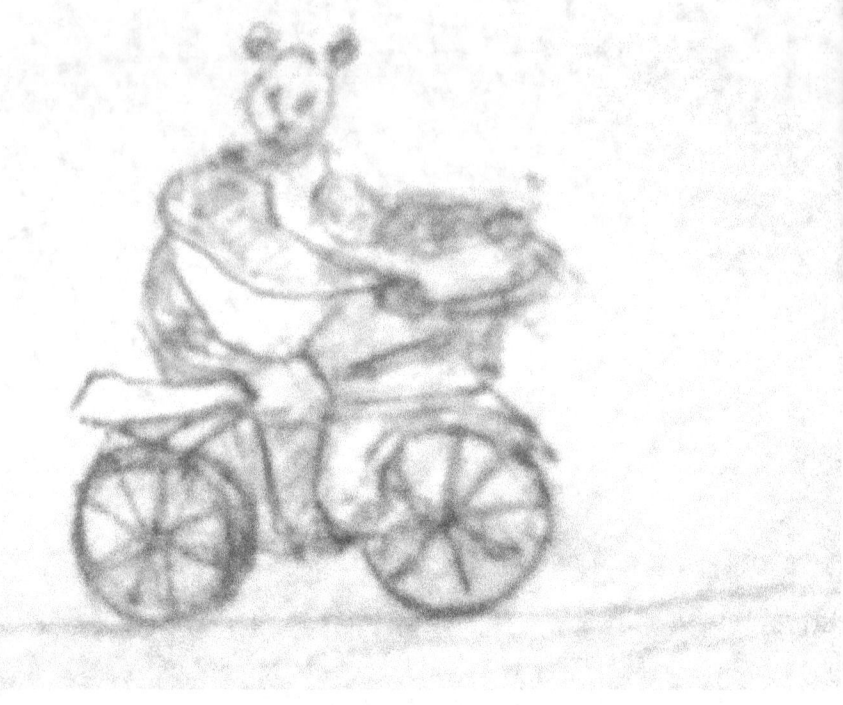

Panda rides bike.

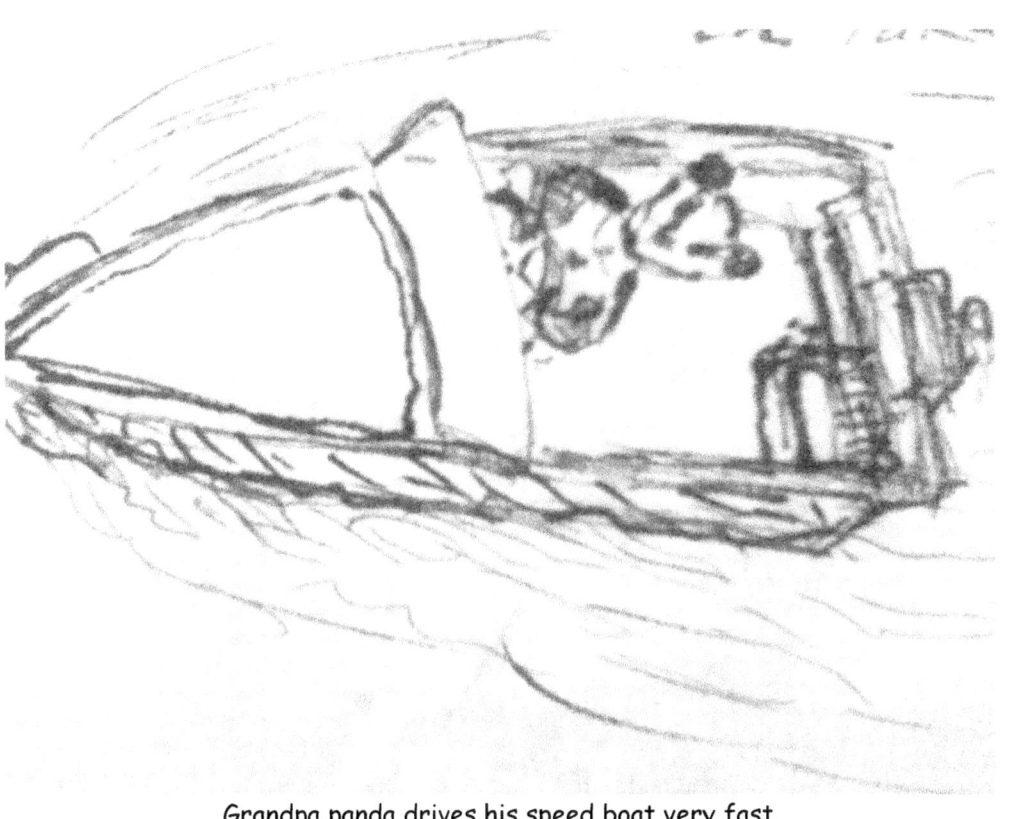

Grandpa panda drives his speed boat very fast.

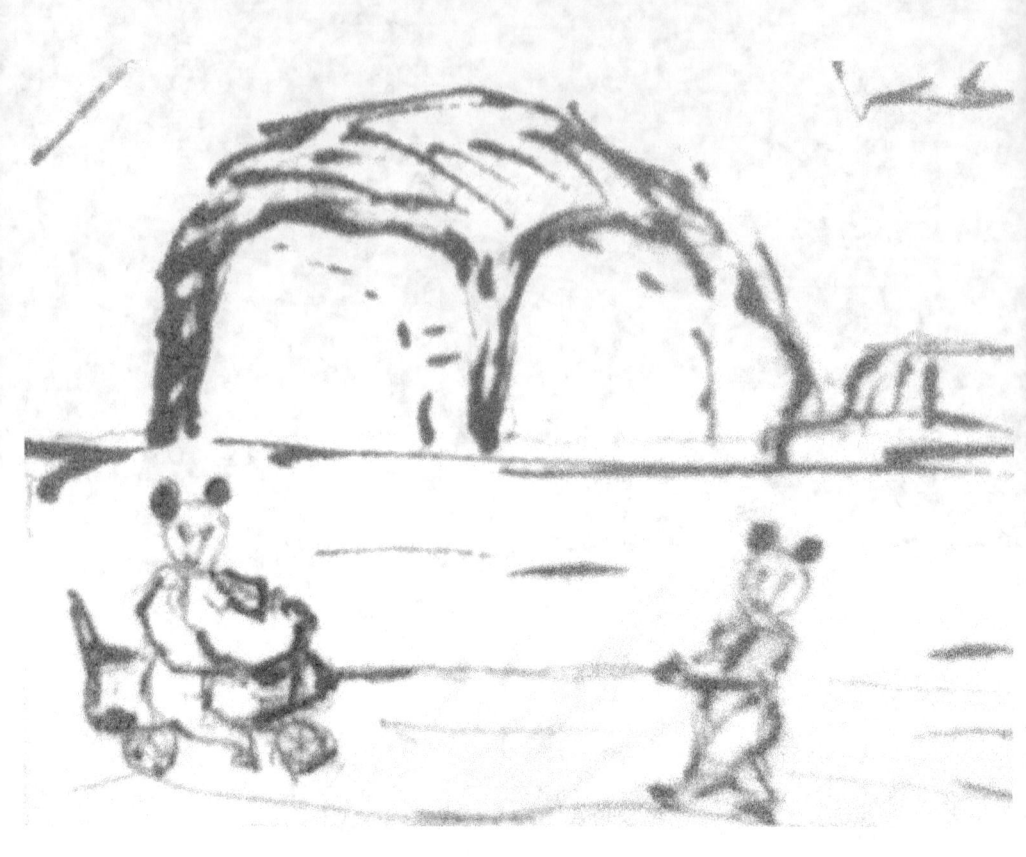

Teen pandas take turns riding scooter.

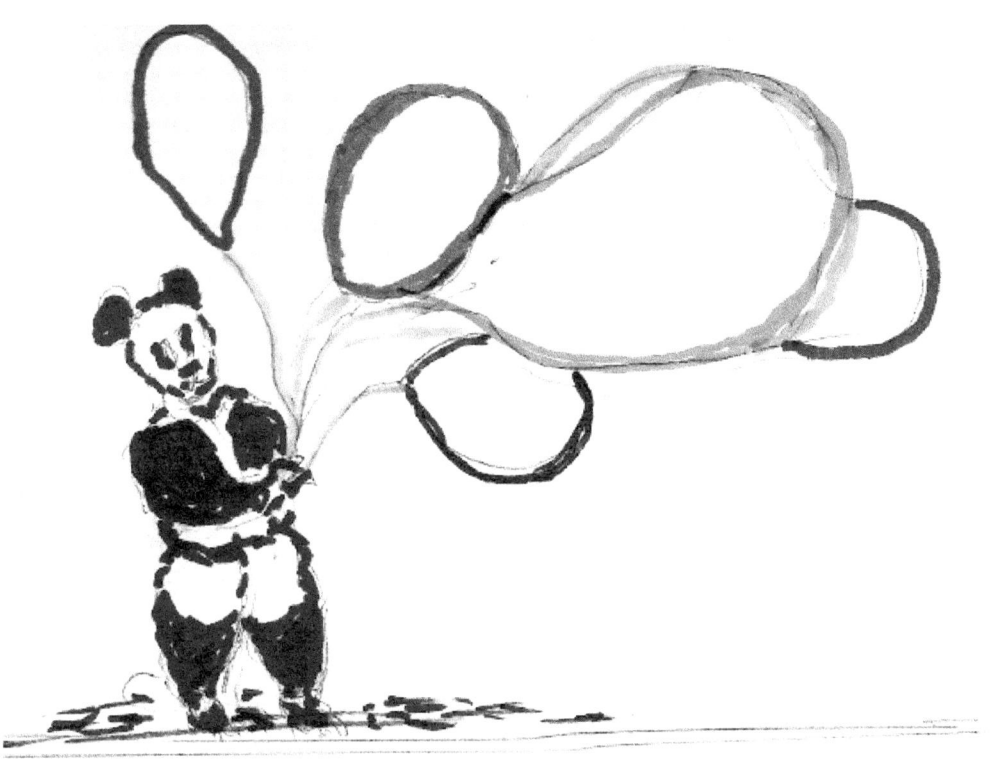

Panda holds a bunch of helium balloons.

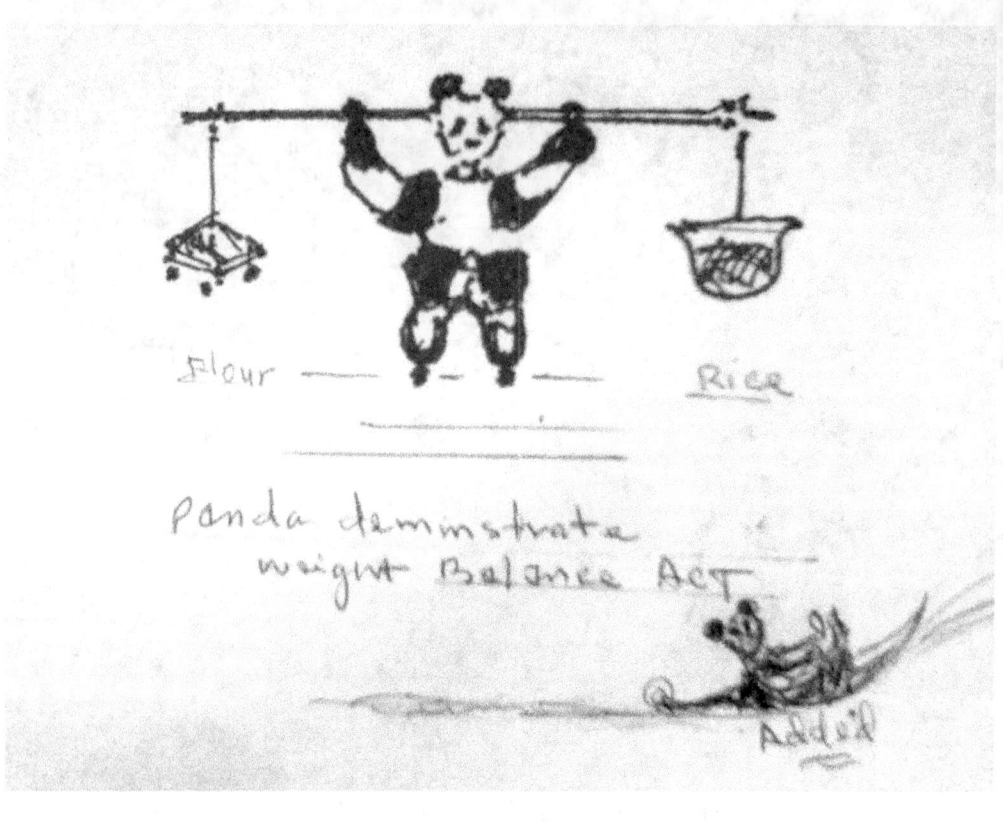

Flour — Rice

Panda demonstrate weight Balance Act

Added

Panda brings flour and rice home from the market. Baby is hungry.

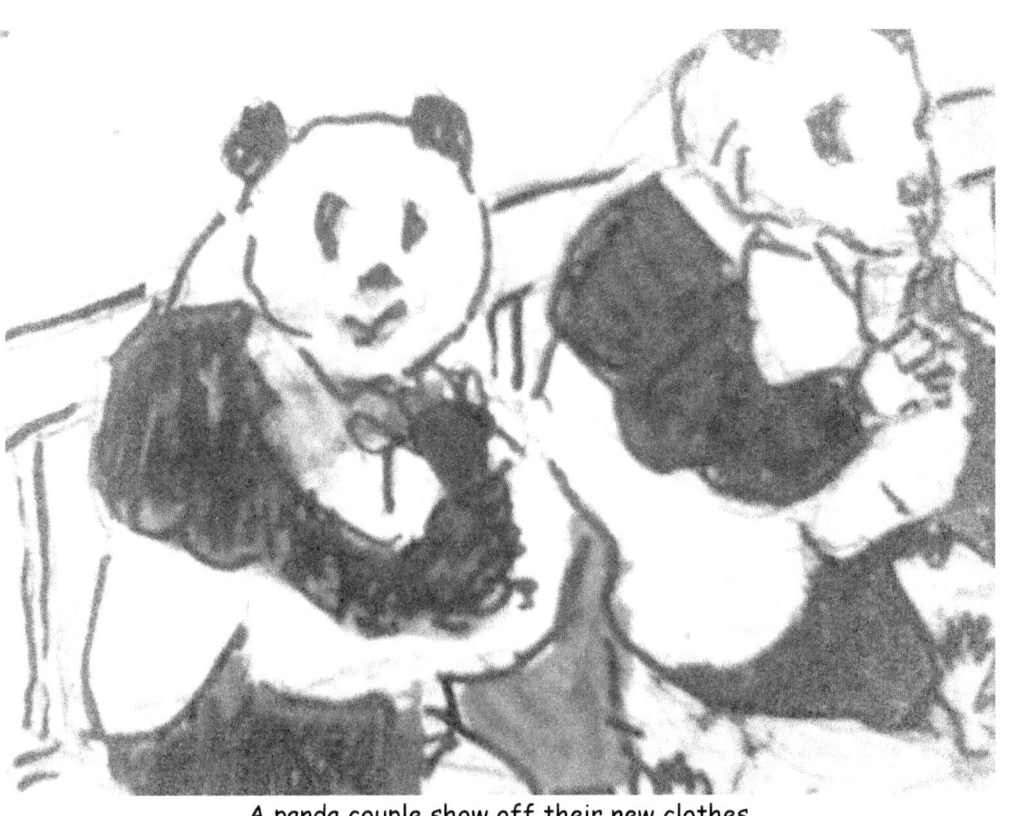

A panda couple show off their new clothes.

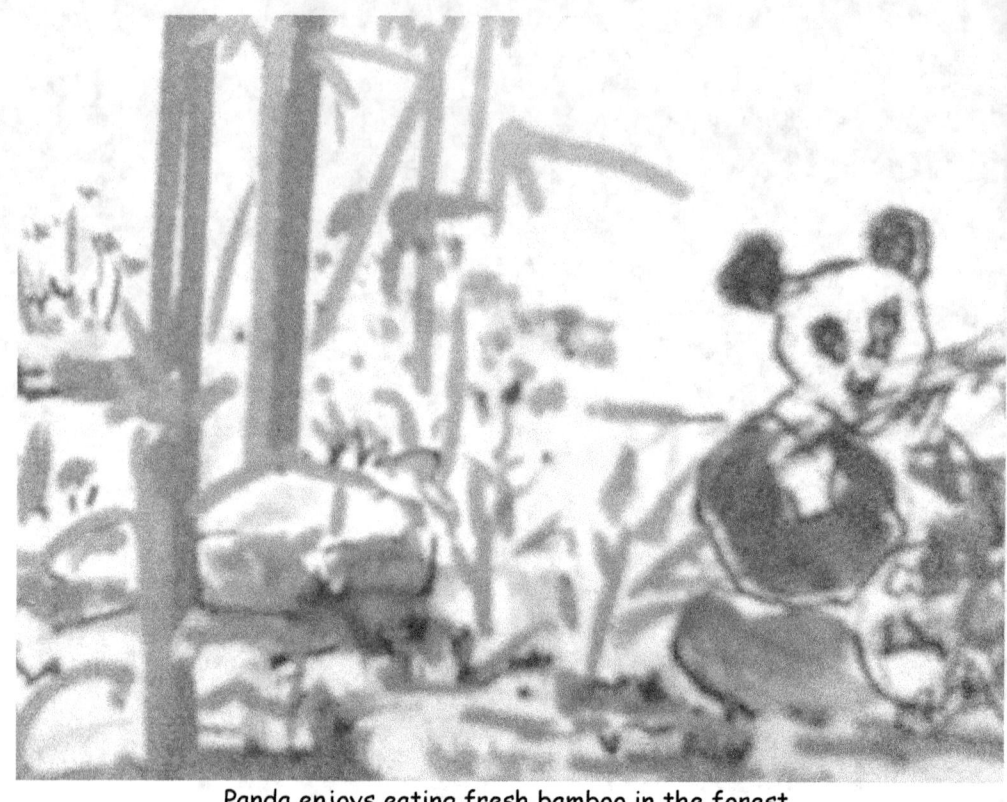

Panda enjoys eating fresh bamboo in the forest.

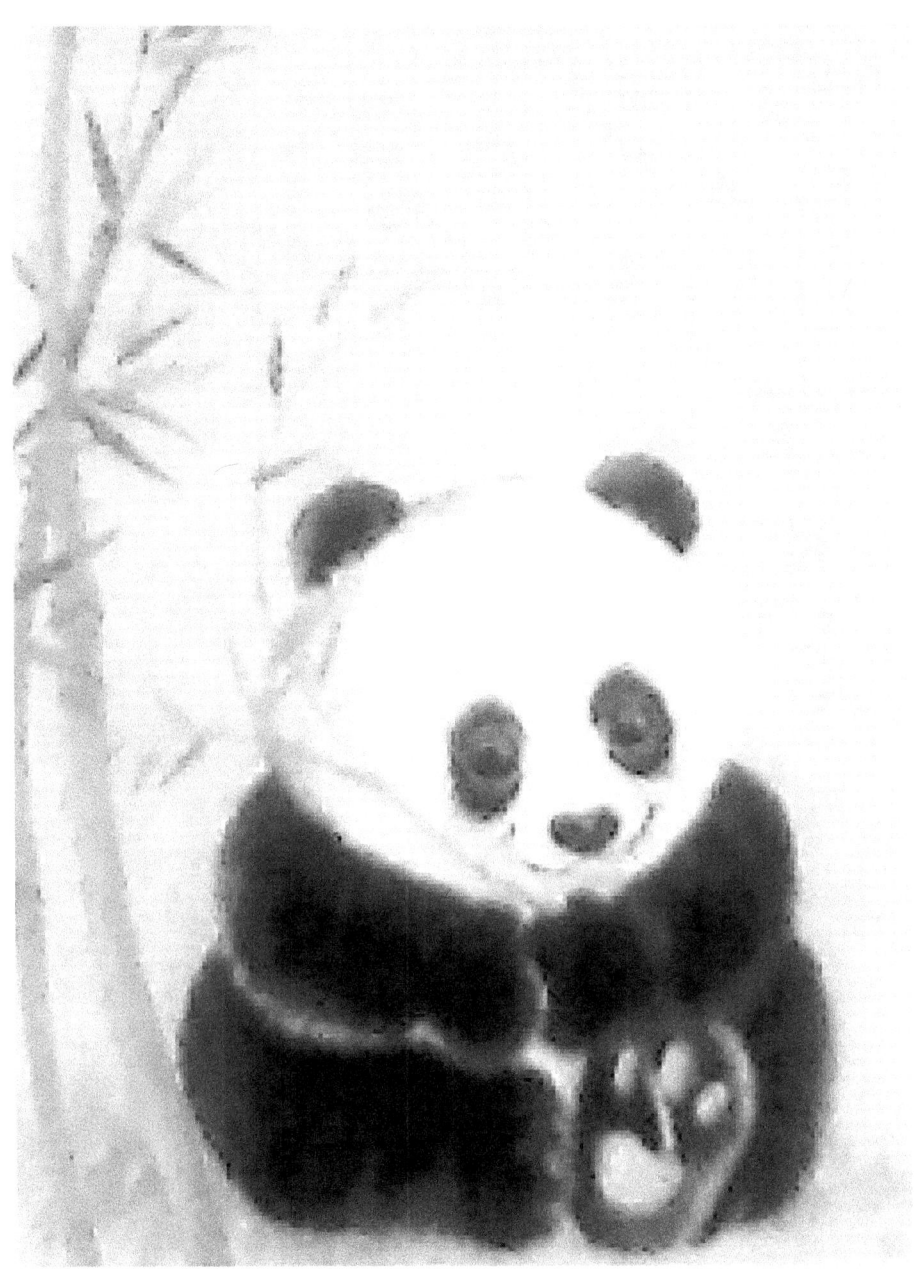

A very happy panda cub plays with bamboo branch.

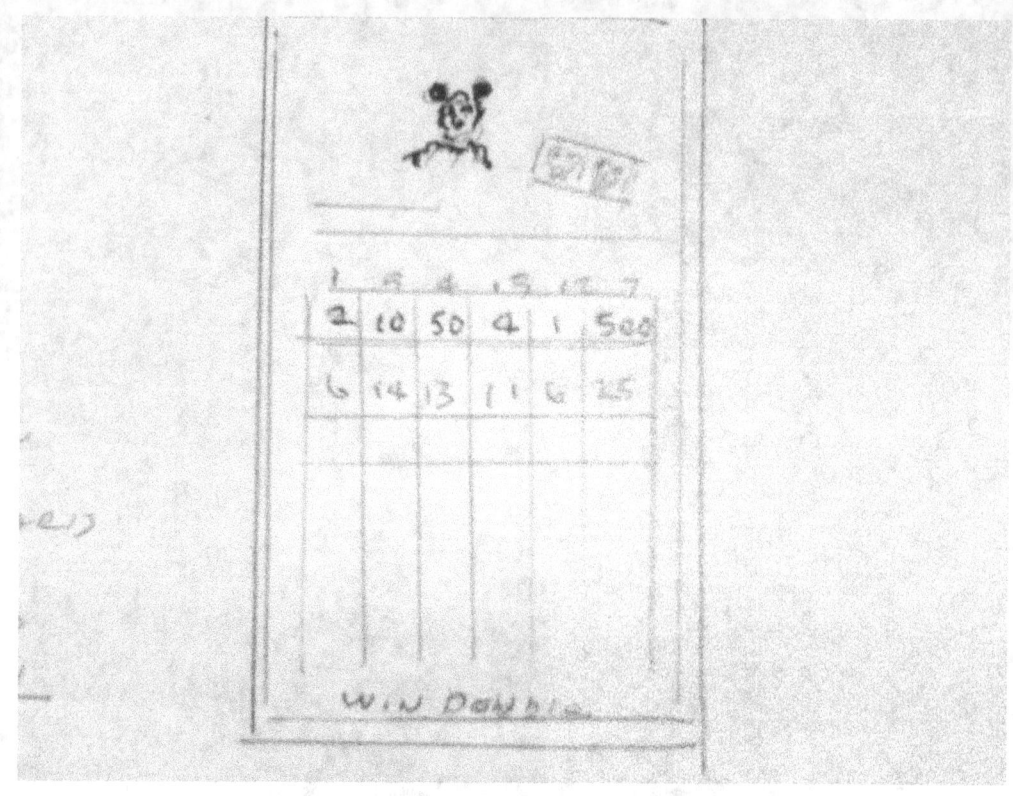

Can panda will the state lottery?

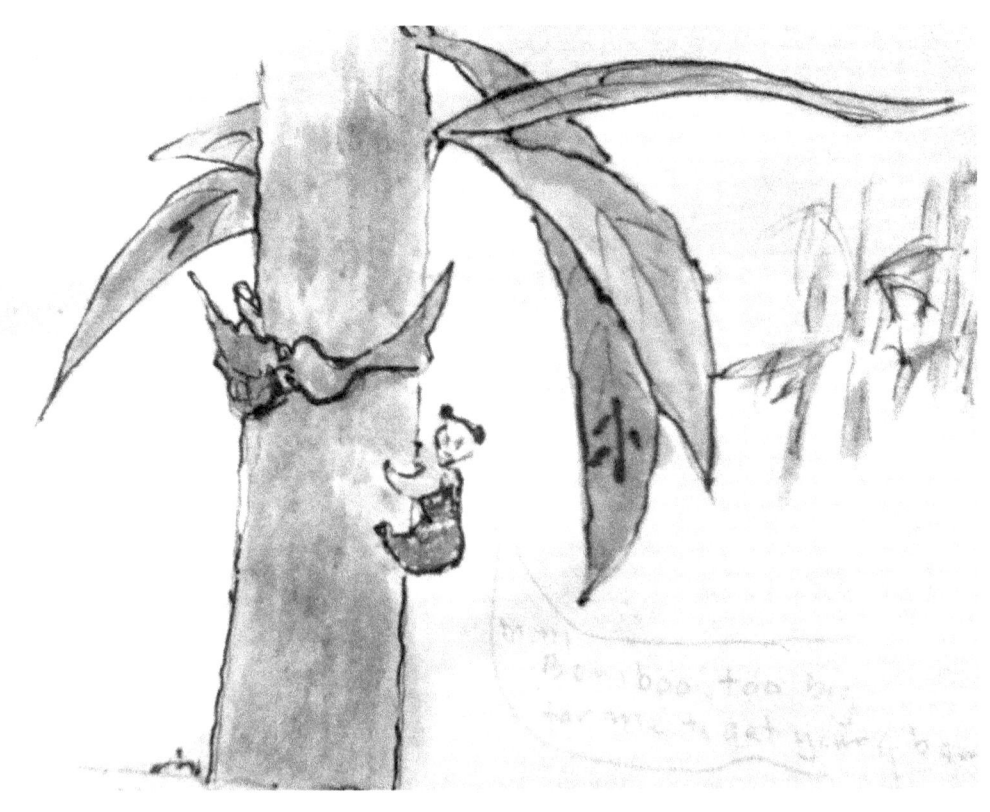

Panda climbs a giant bamboo tree.

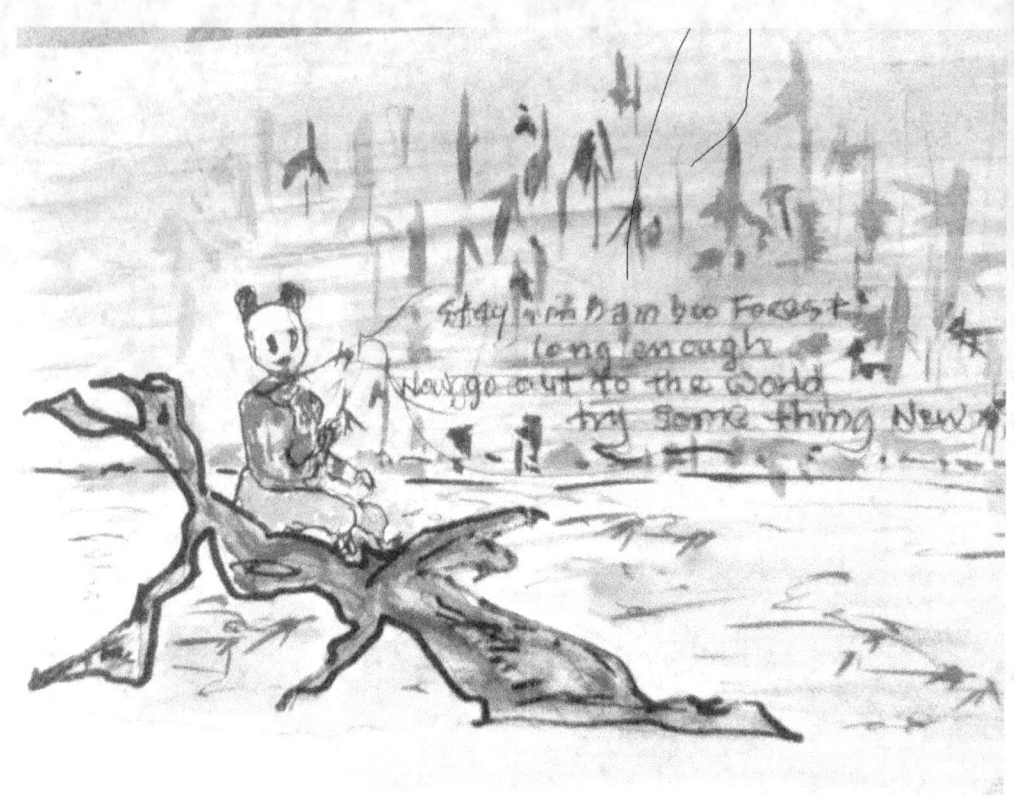

Girl panda thinking about her future outside of the bamboo forest.

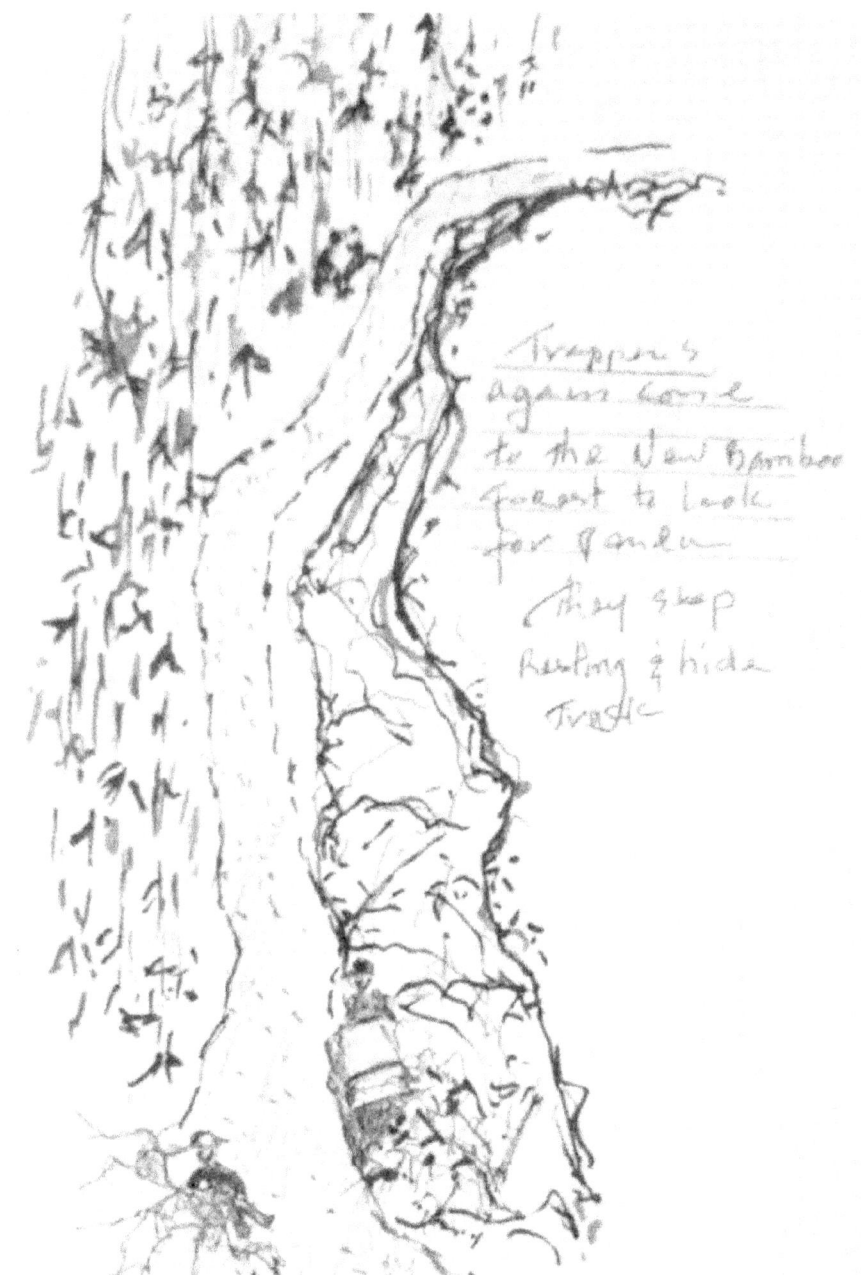

A panda cub climbs high up a giant bamboo tree to flee trappers.

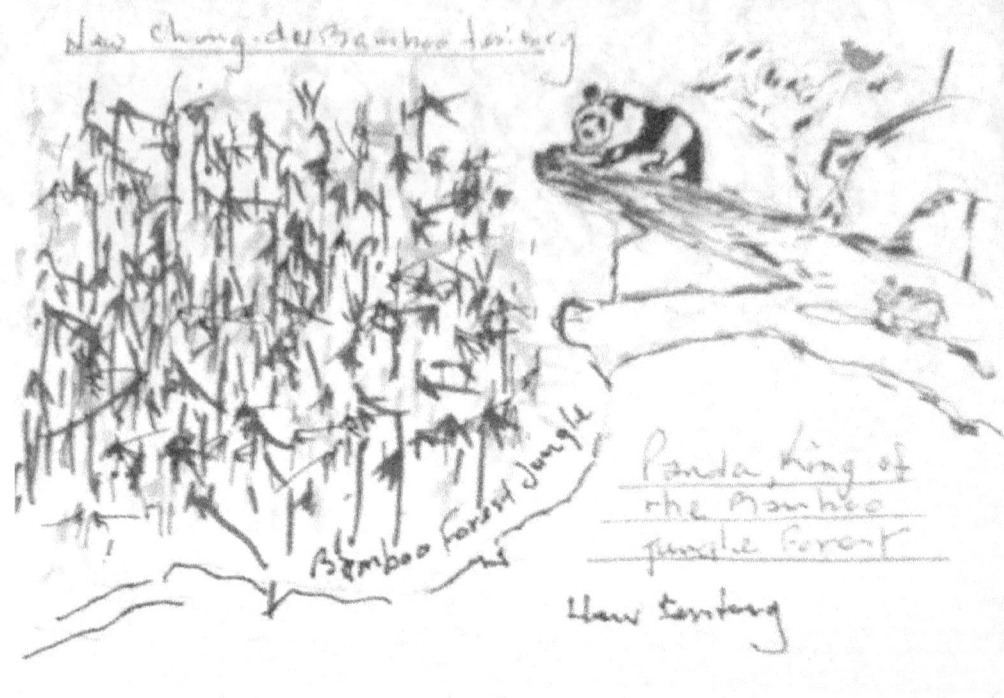

Panda see panda forest below standing on a log high up on a cliff.

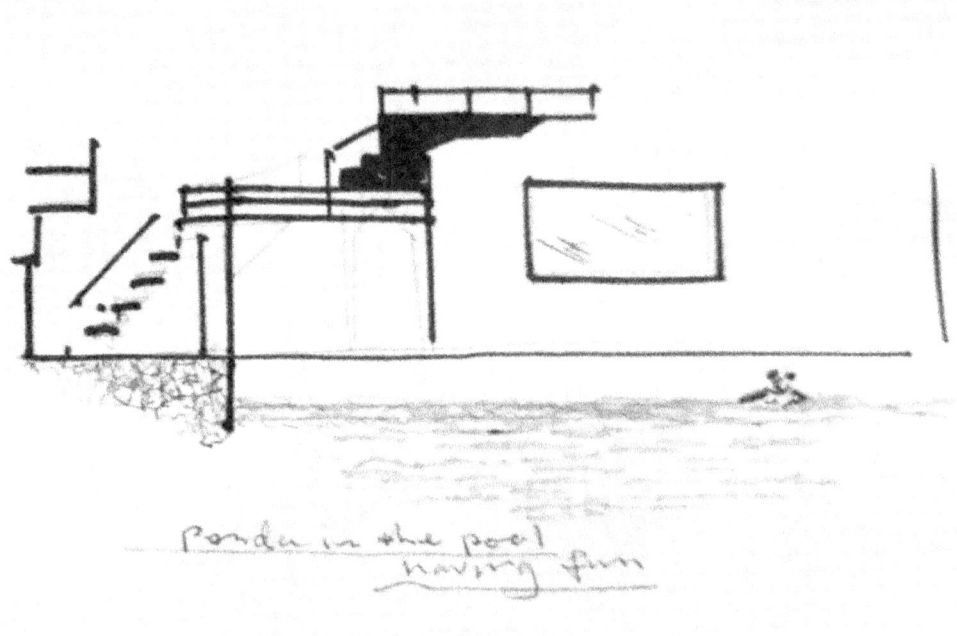

Panda swims in pool while homeowners are away.

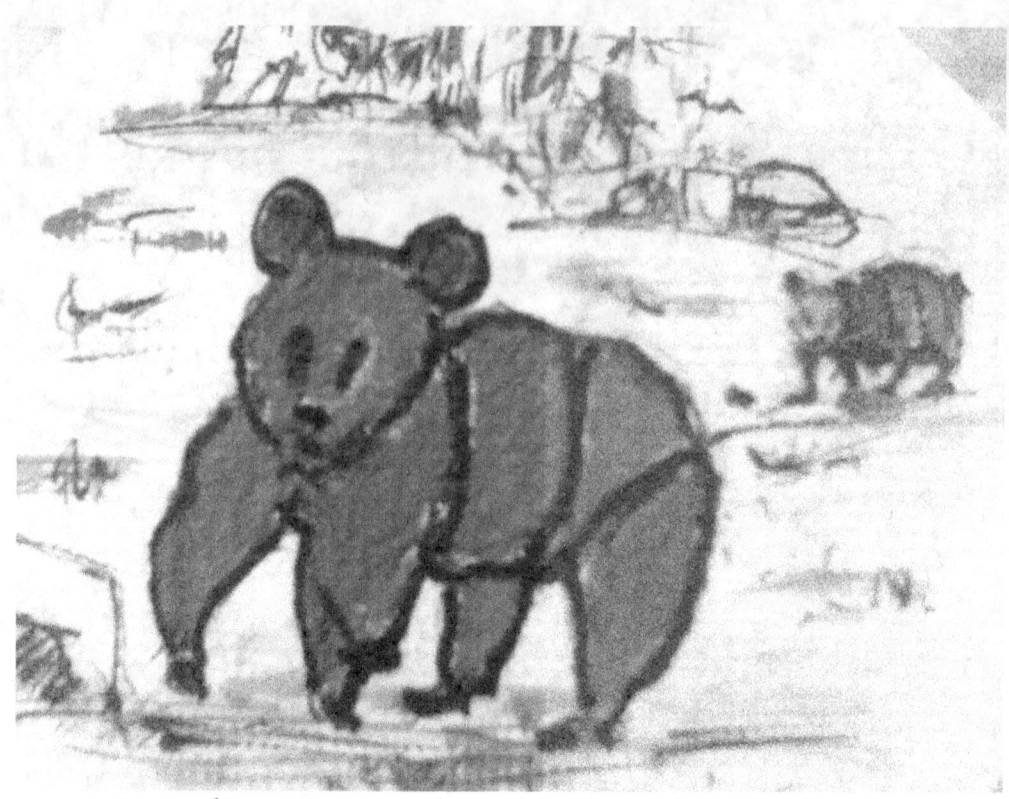

A pair of brown bears wander near by the panda bamboo forest.

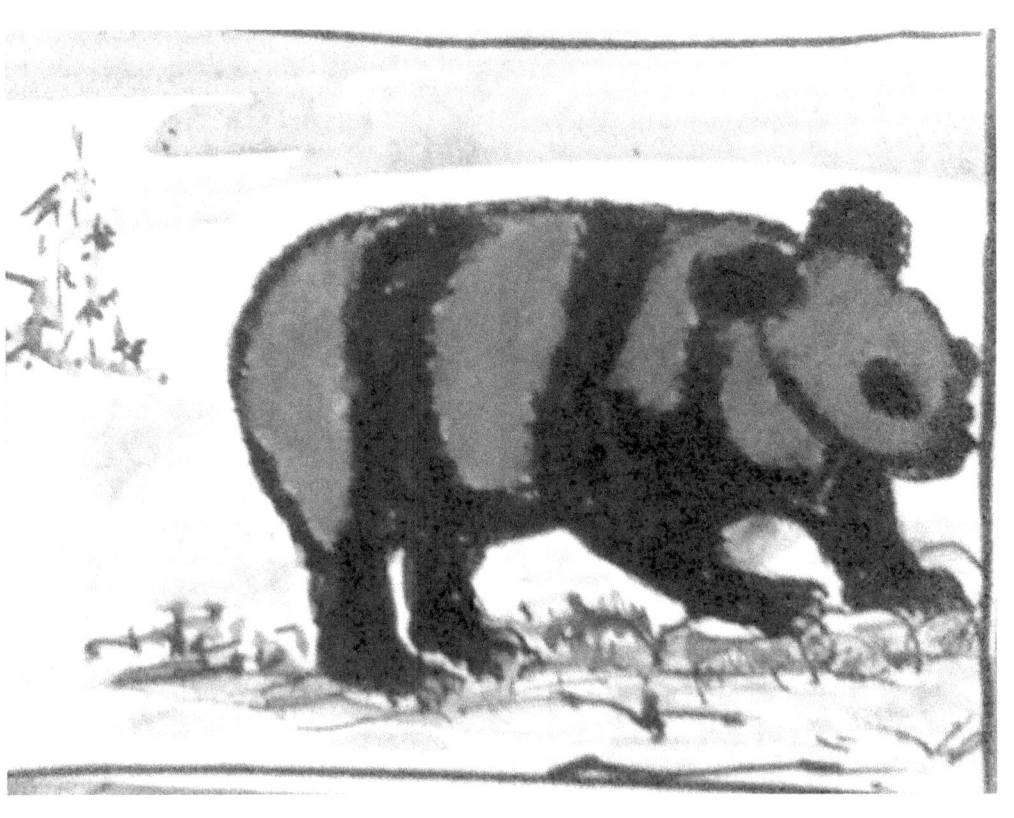

A panda – brown bear hybrid eats both veggies and meat.

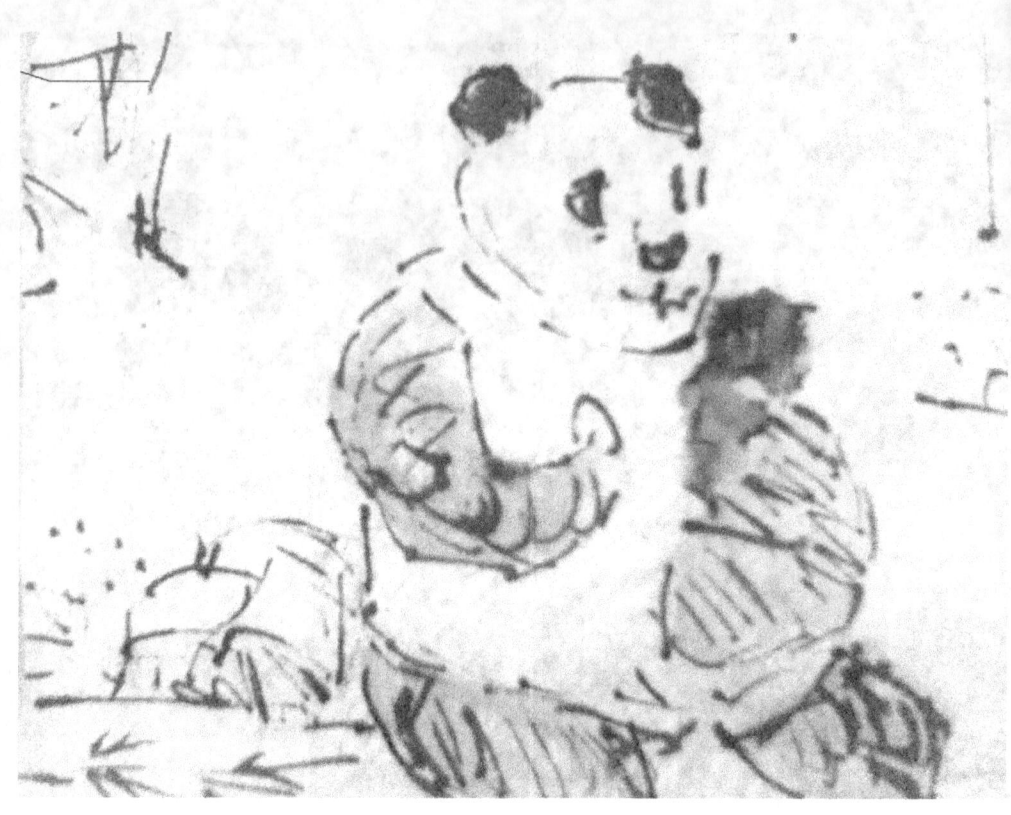

Panda holds pet cat on its arm.

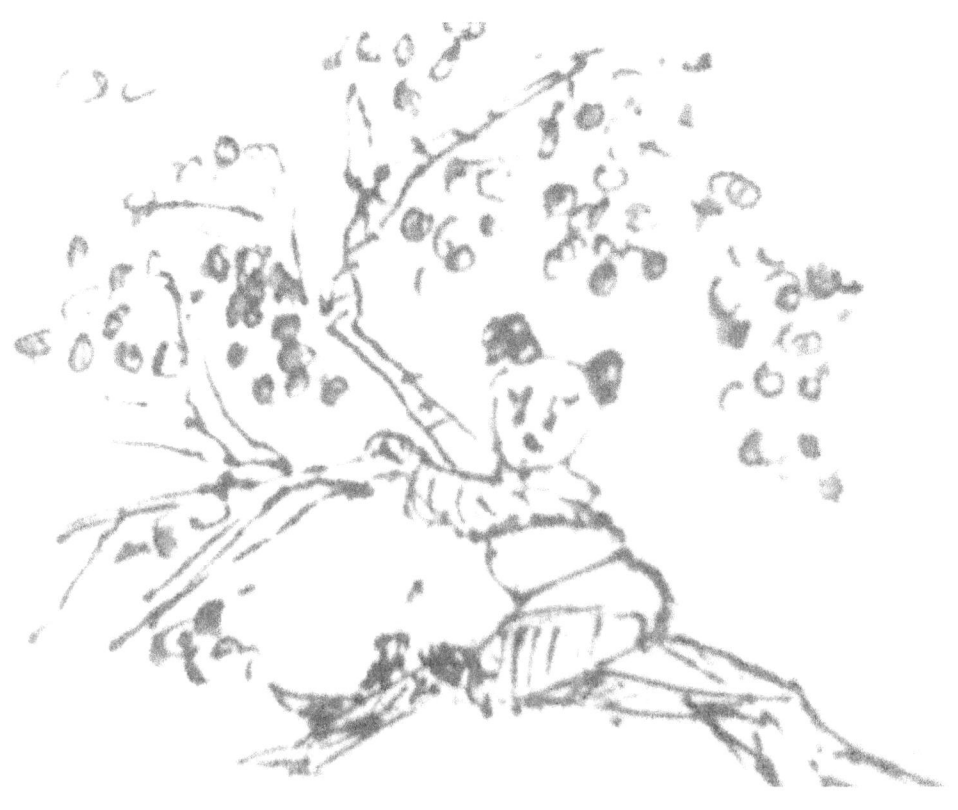

Girl panda climbs apple tree to get some fruit.

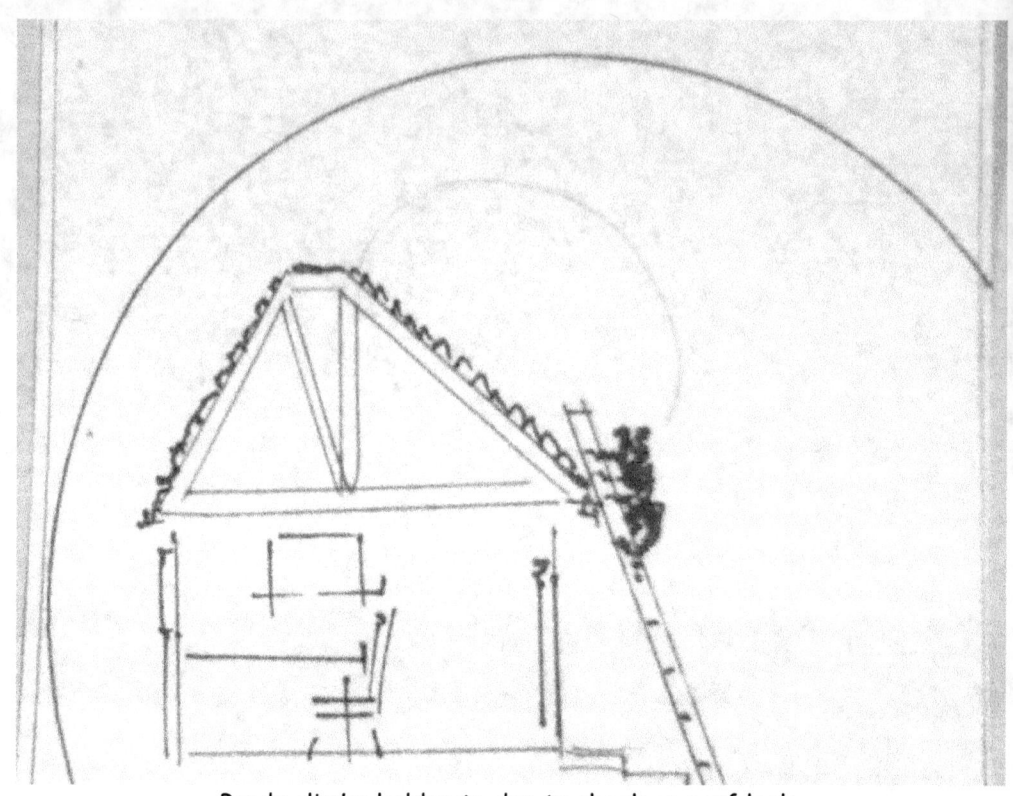

Panda climbs ladder to den to check on roof leak.

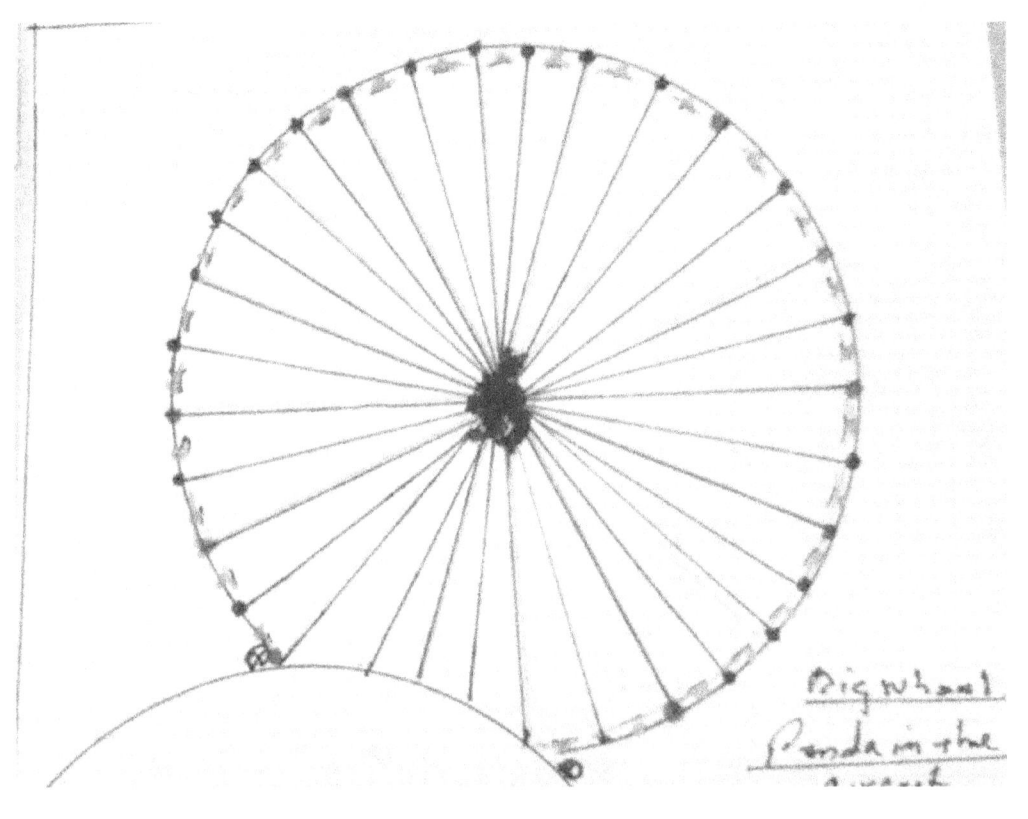

A panda works the Ferris wheel at the amusement park.

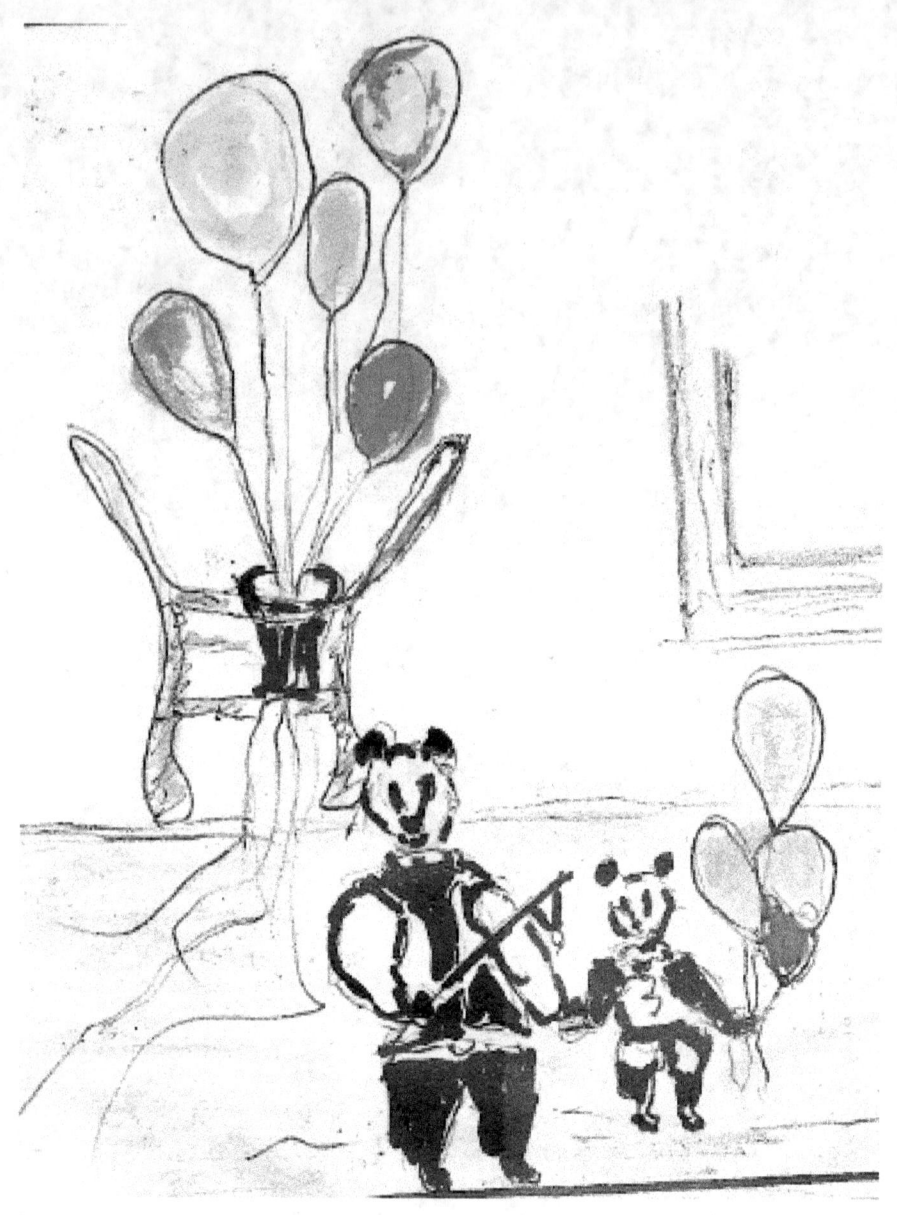

Mother panda buys her cub some helium balloons.

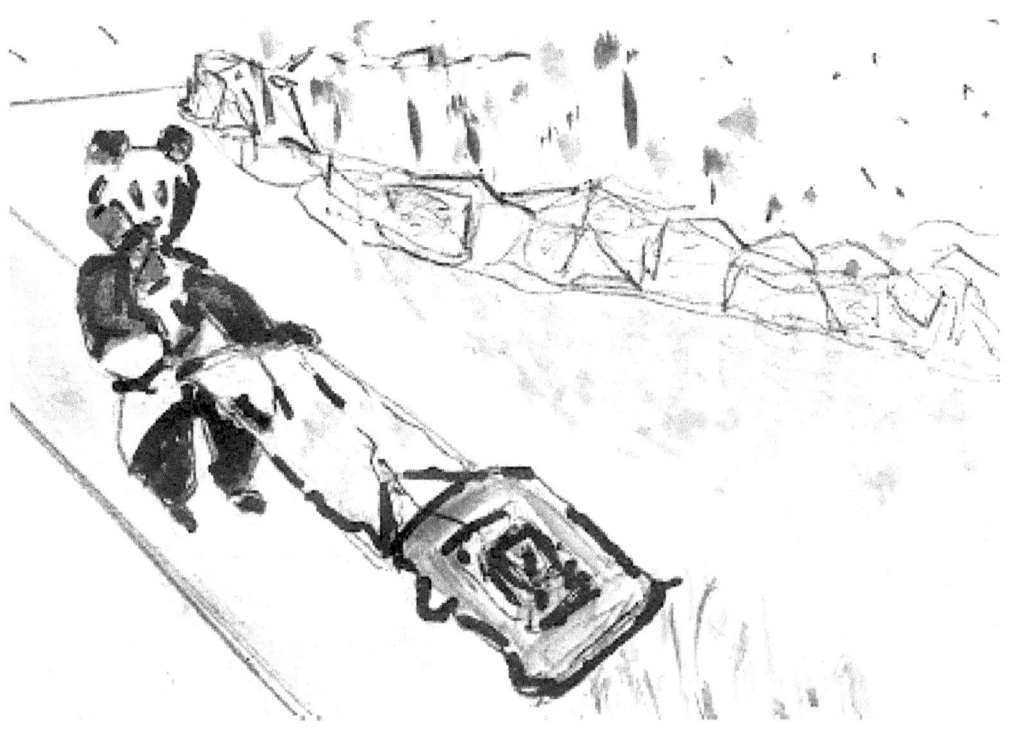

Teen panda mows lawn while talking on a cell phone.

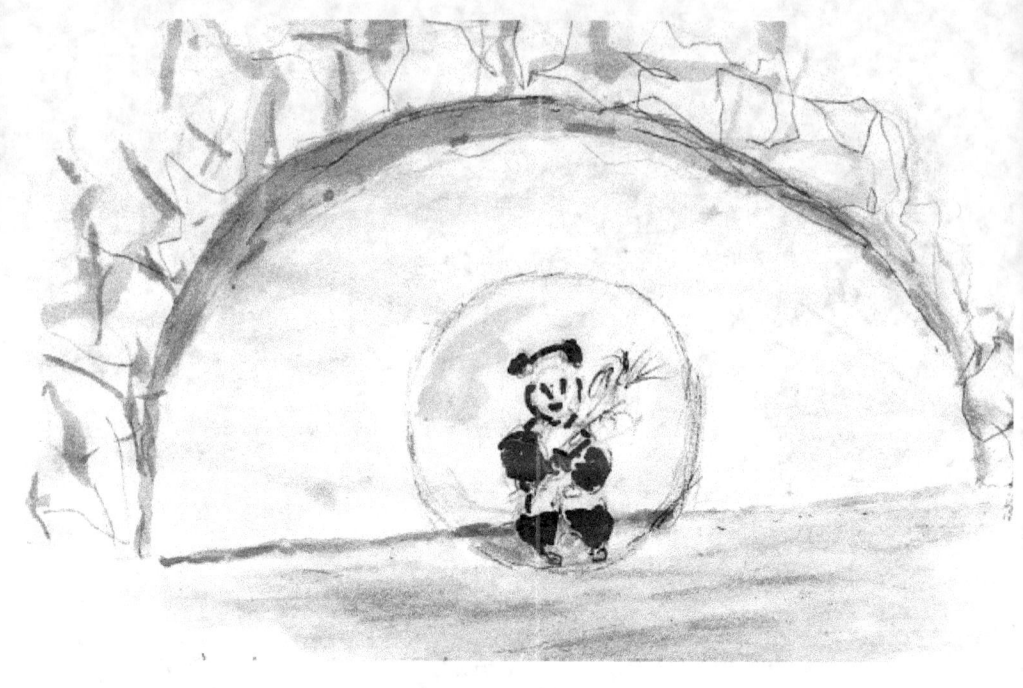

Panda enjoys bamboo under an arch while floating in a bubble on the water.

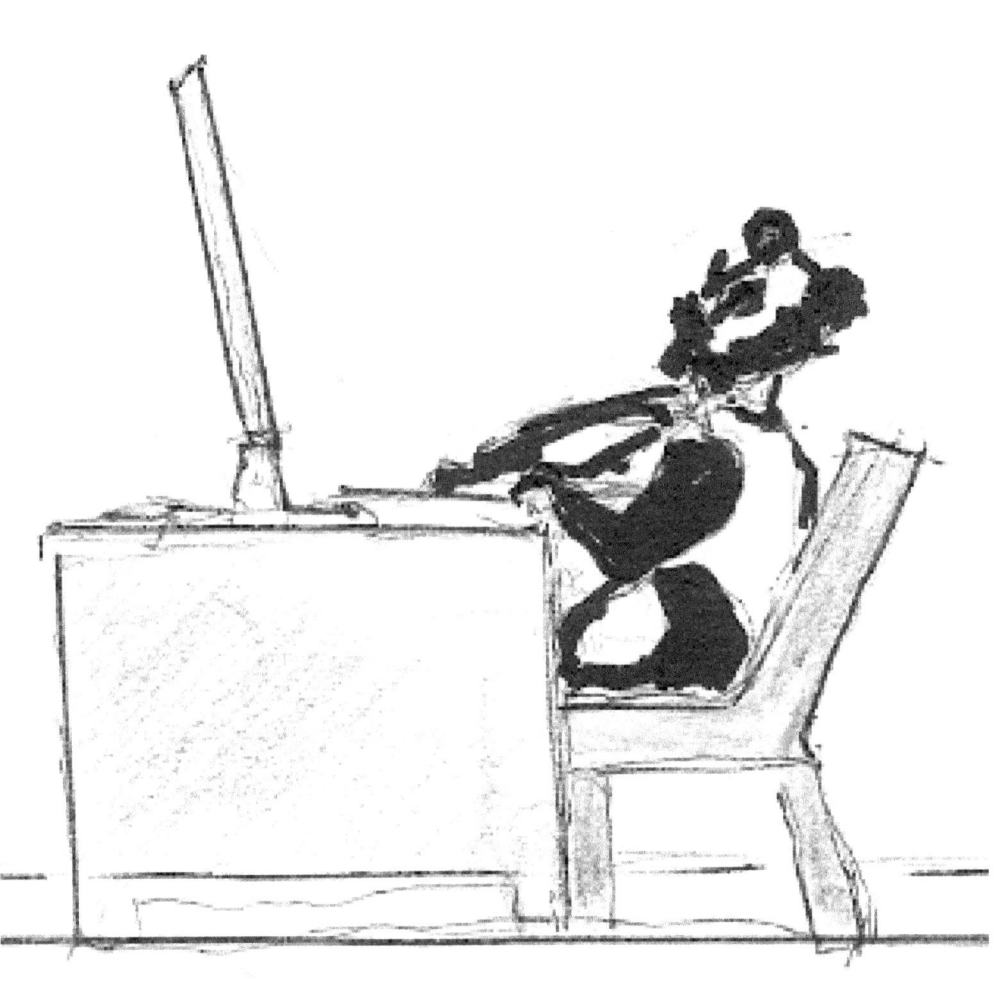

Grandpa panda is enjoying social media on the Internet.

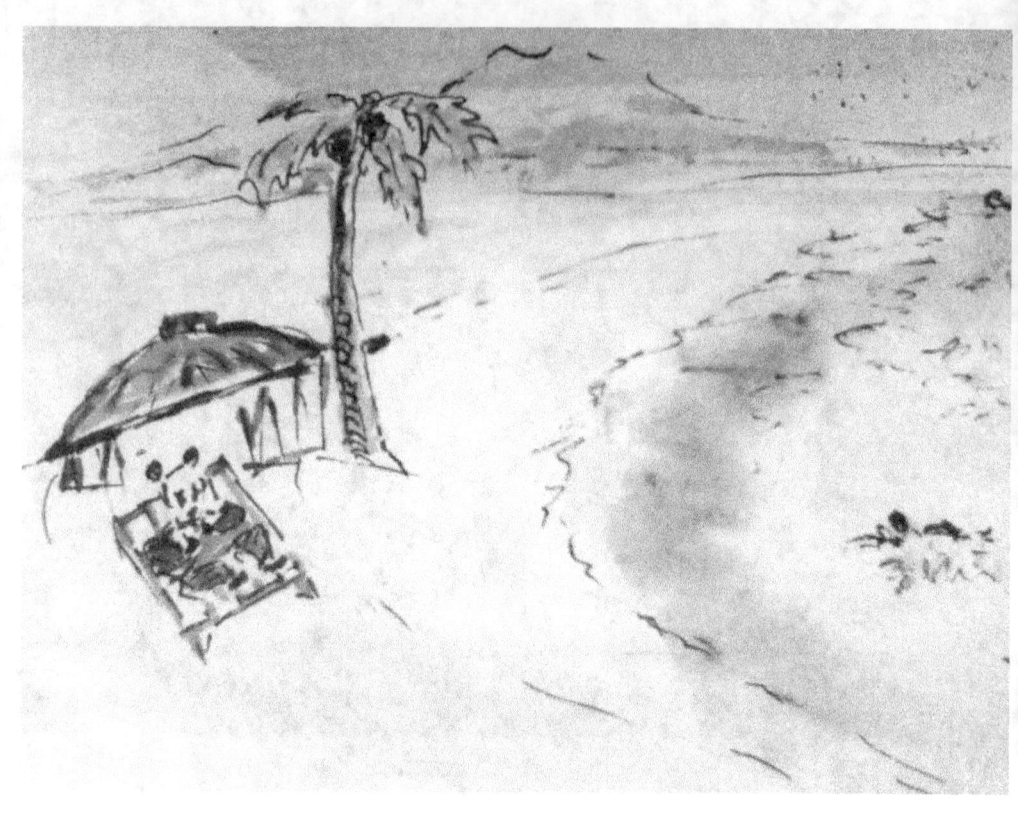

Panda enjoys laying out at the beach.

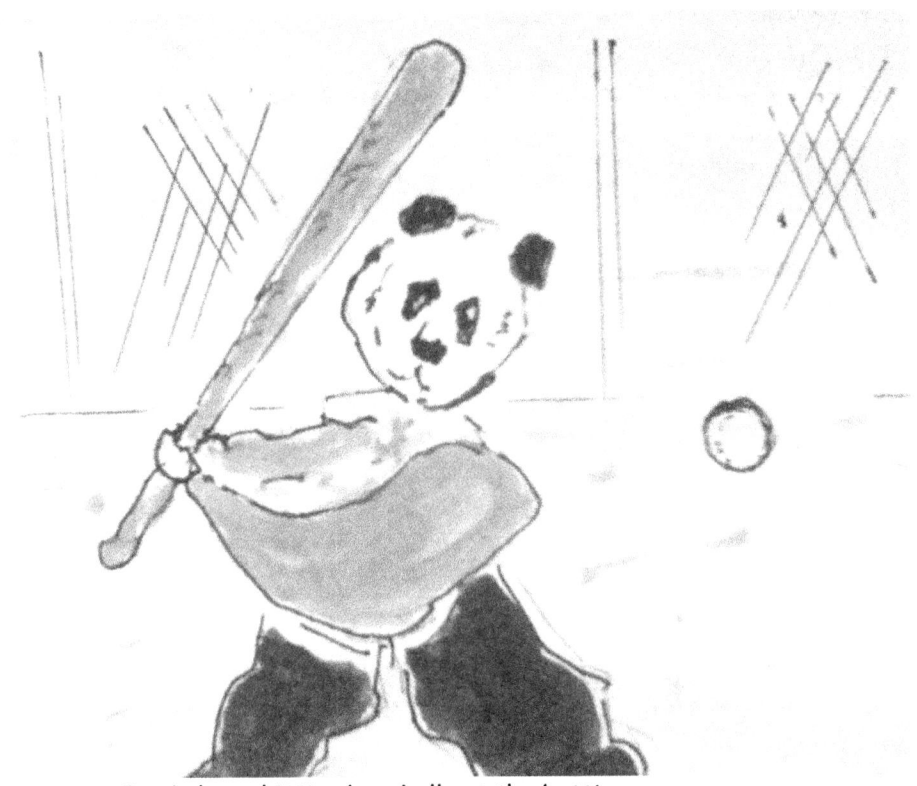

Panda loves hitting baseballs at the batting cage.

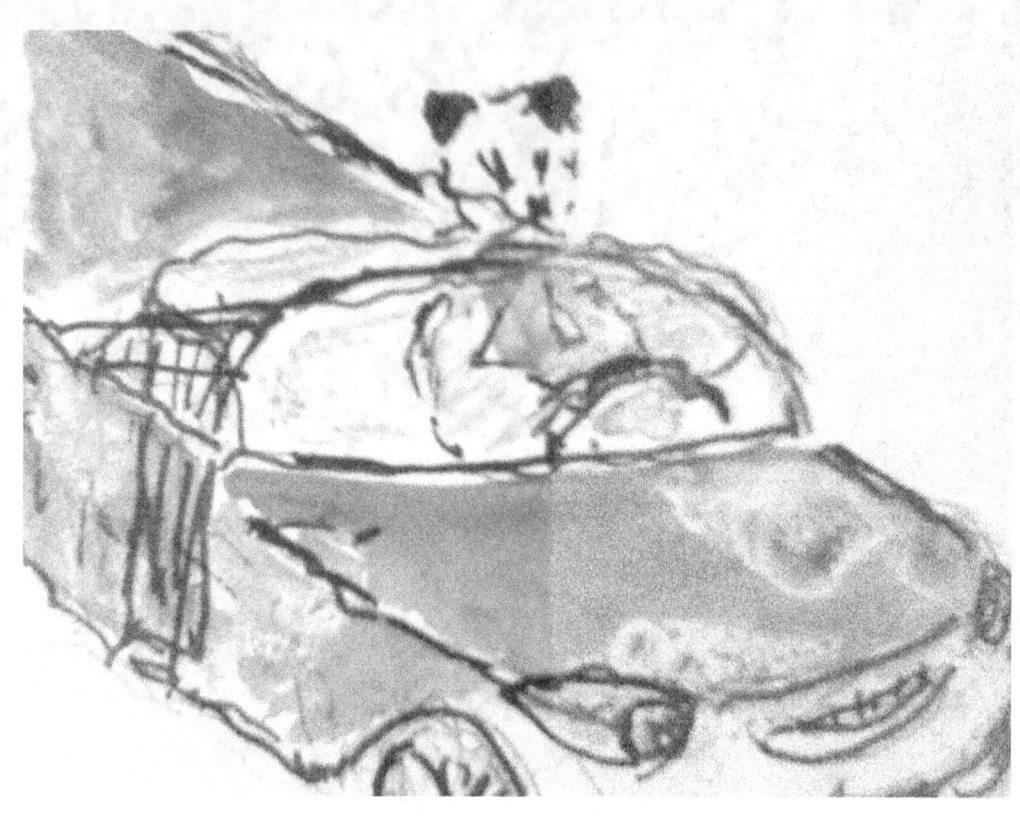

Panda enjoys driving fast.

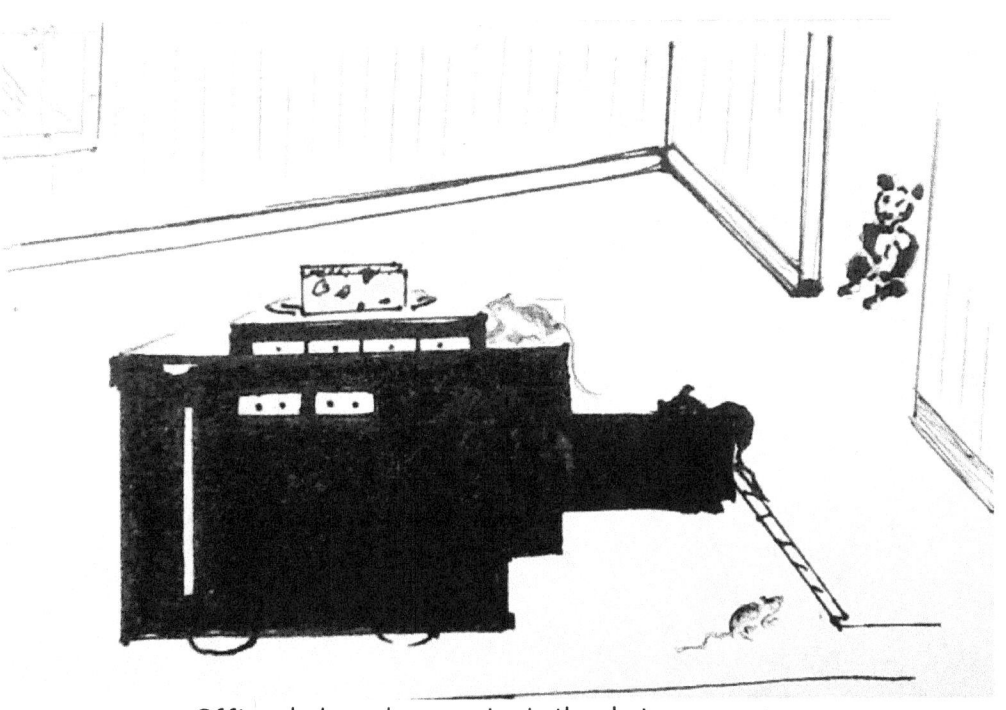

Office clerk panda sees mice in the photo copy room.

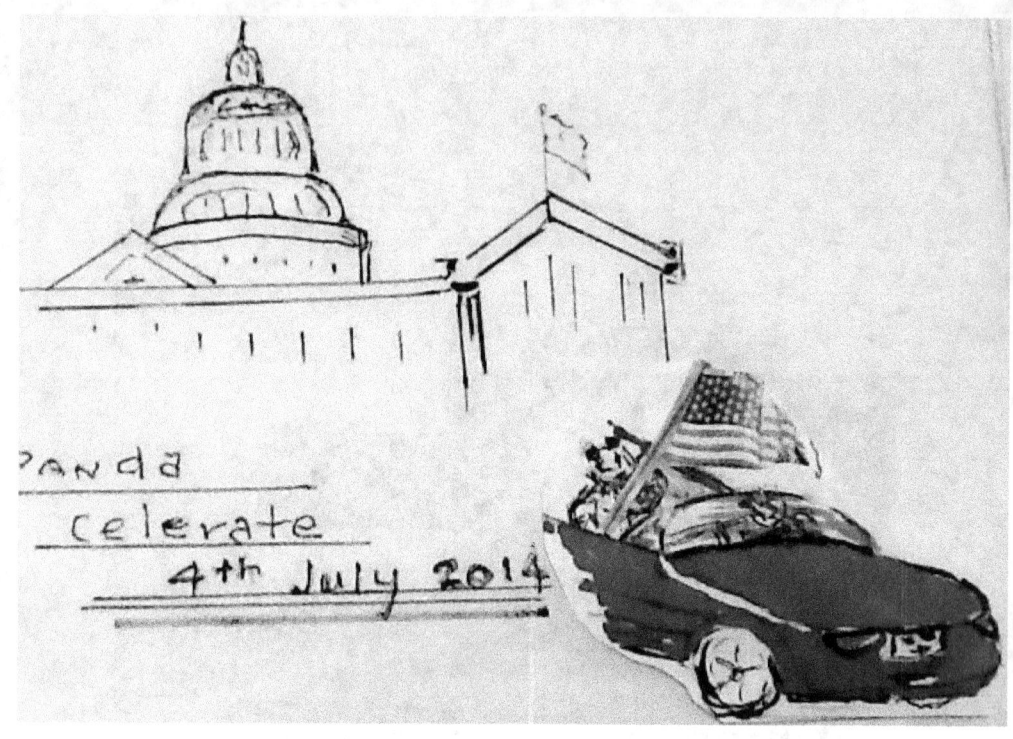

Patriotic panda celebrates the Fourth of July.

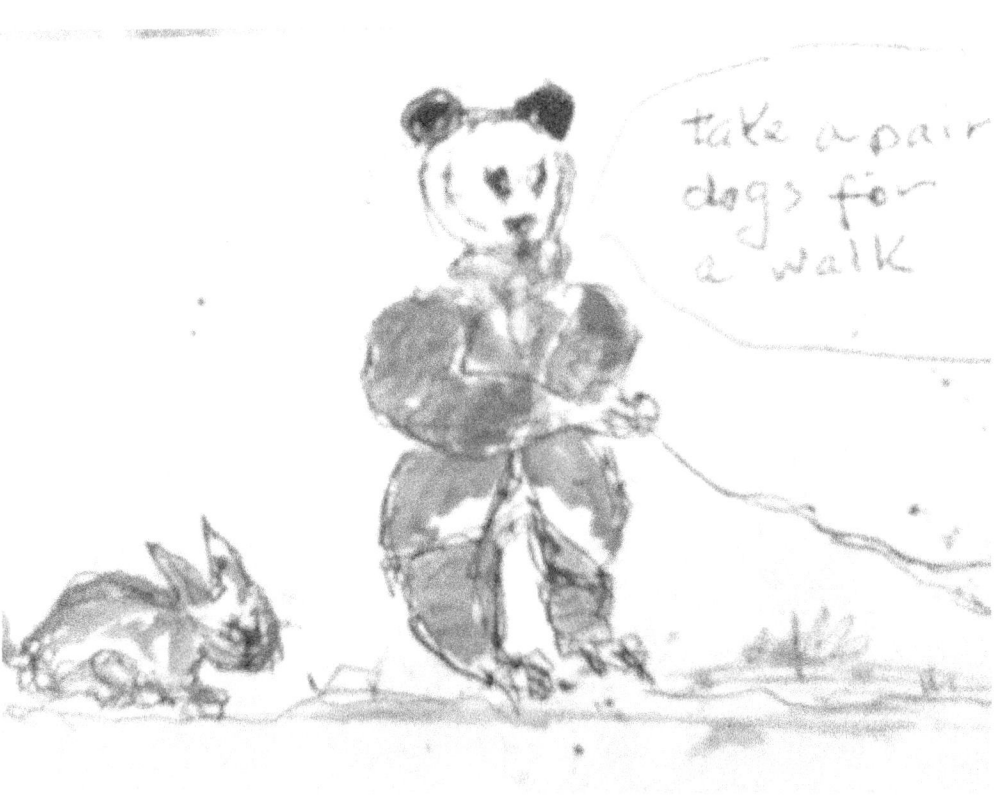

Girl panda takes rabbit for a hop... but she thinks it's a dog.

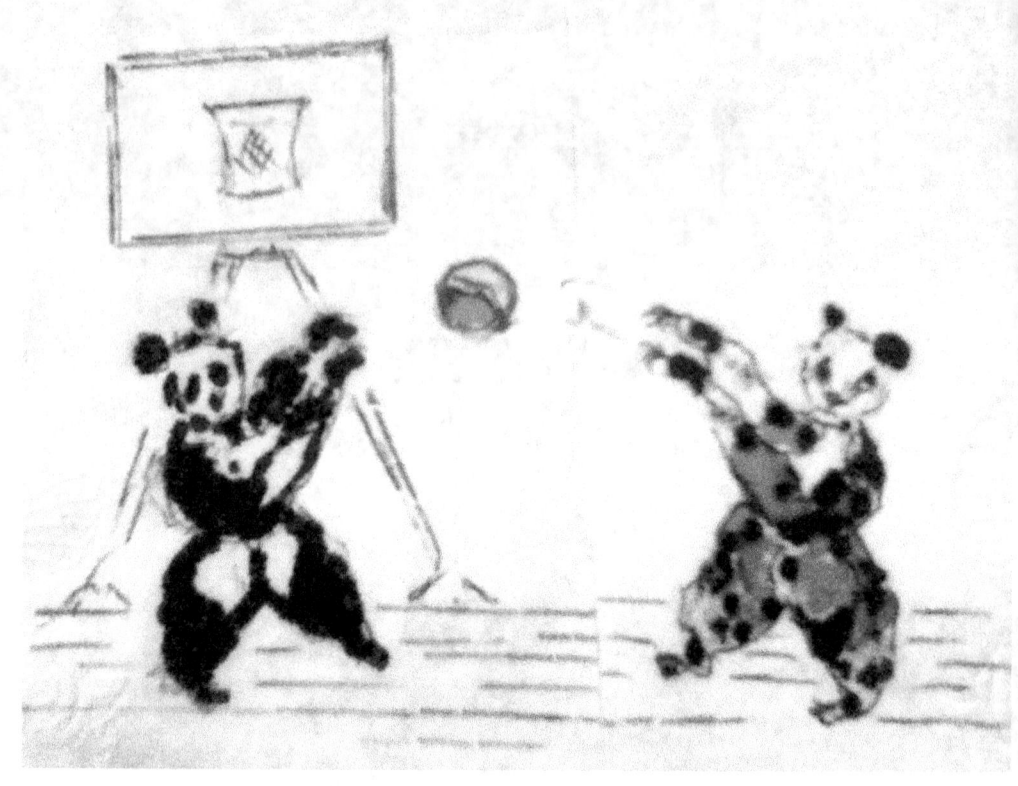

Pandas play "one-on-one" basketball.

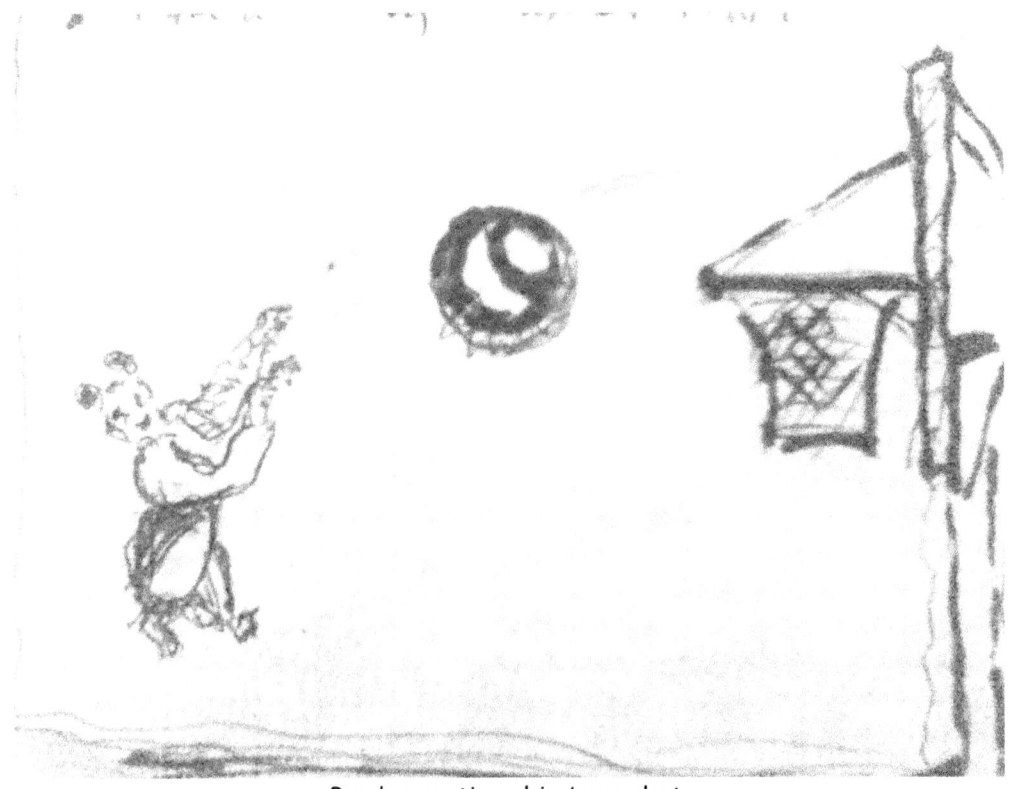

Panda practices his jump shot.

www.ingramcontent.com/pod-product-compliance
Lightning Source LLC
Chambersburg PA
CBHW060148200526
45165CB00023B/1330